Picture book of

FUNNY ANIMALS

CUTE AND HILARIOUS PHOTOS

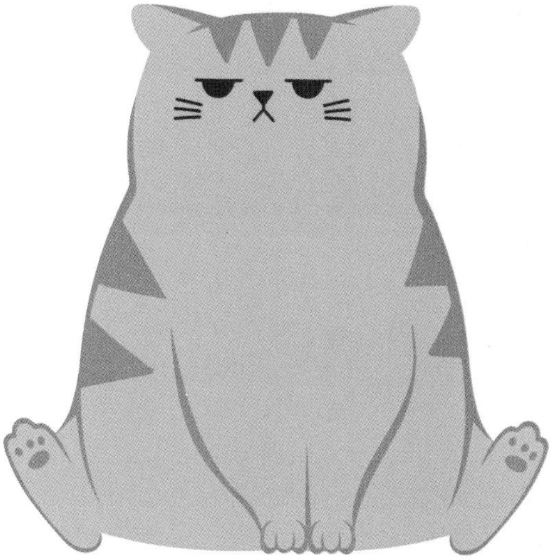

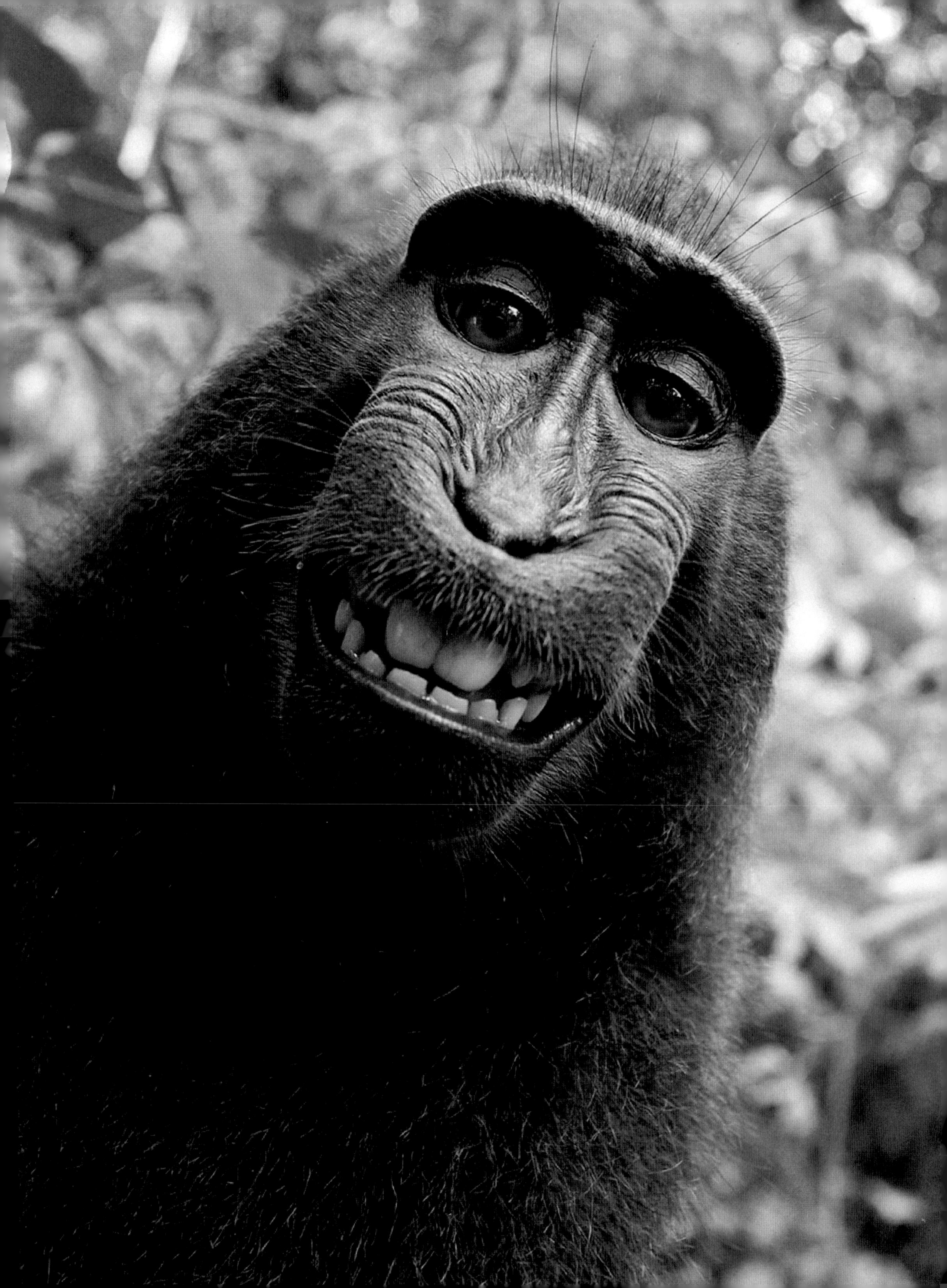

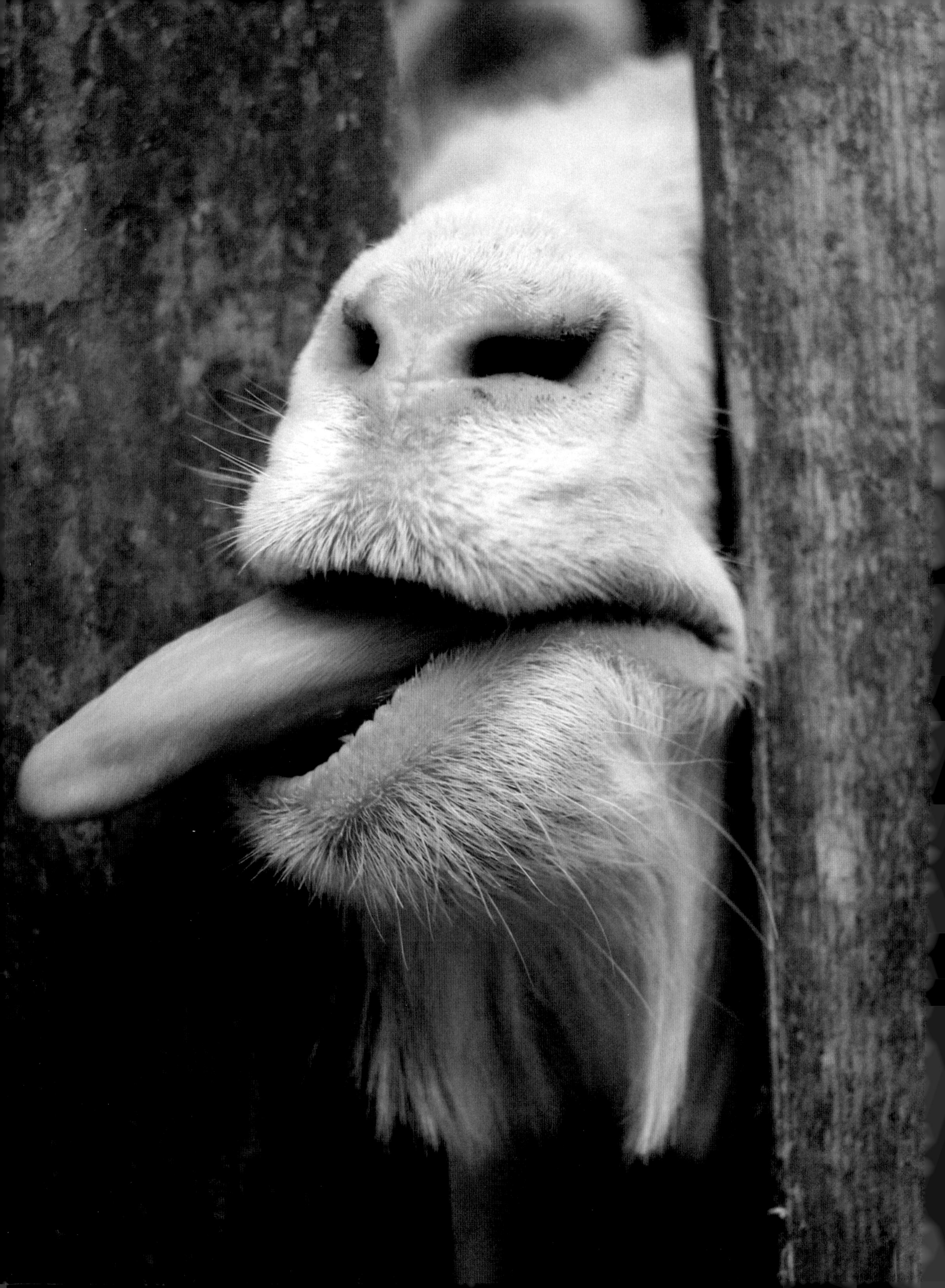

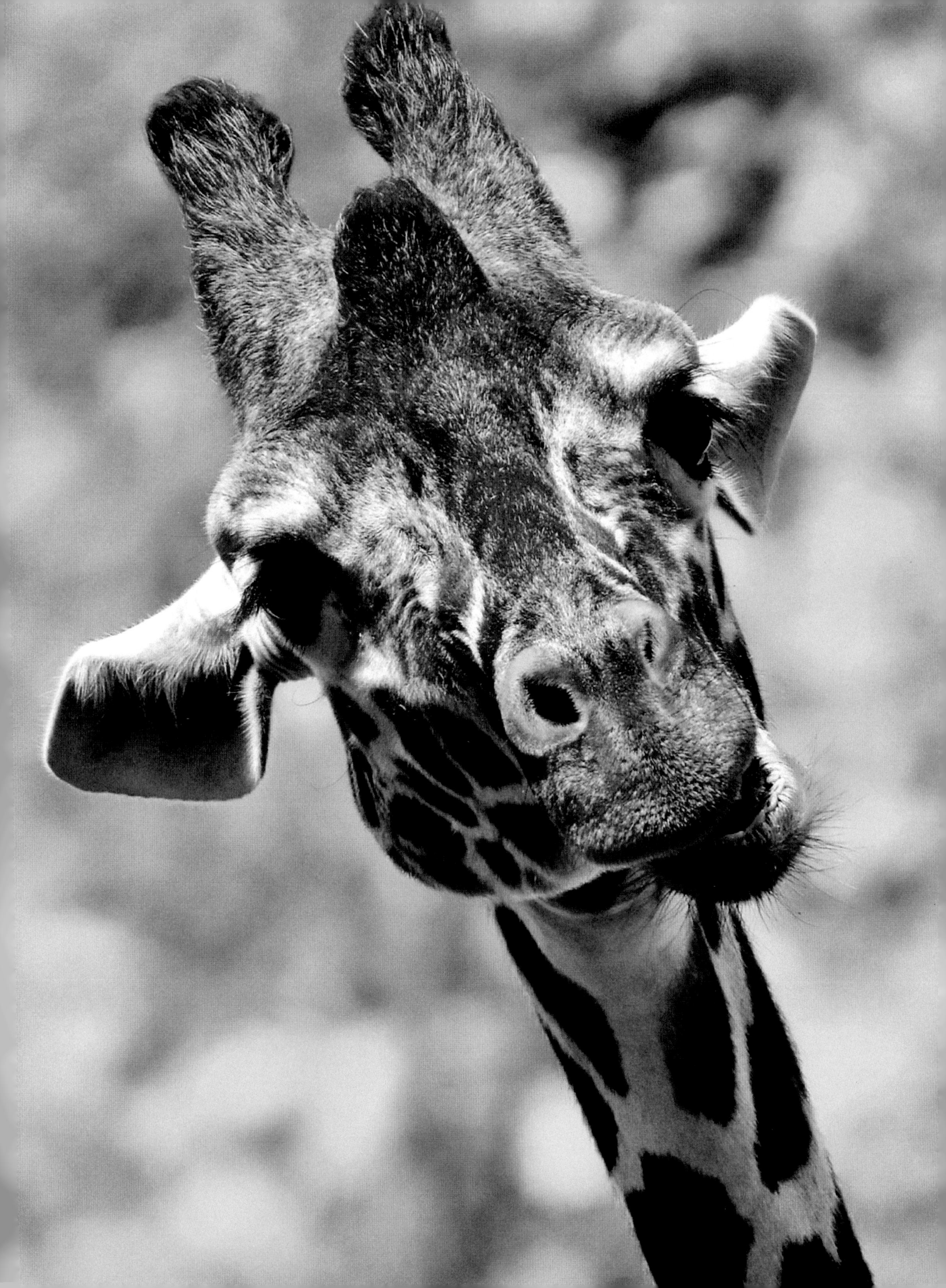

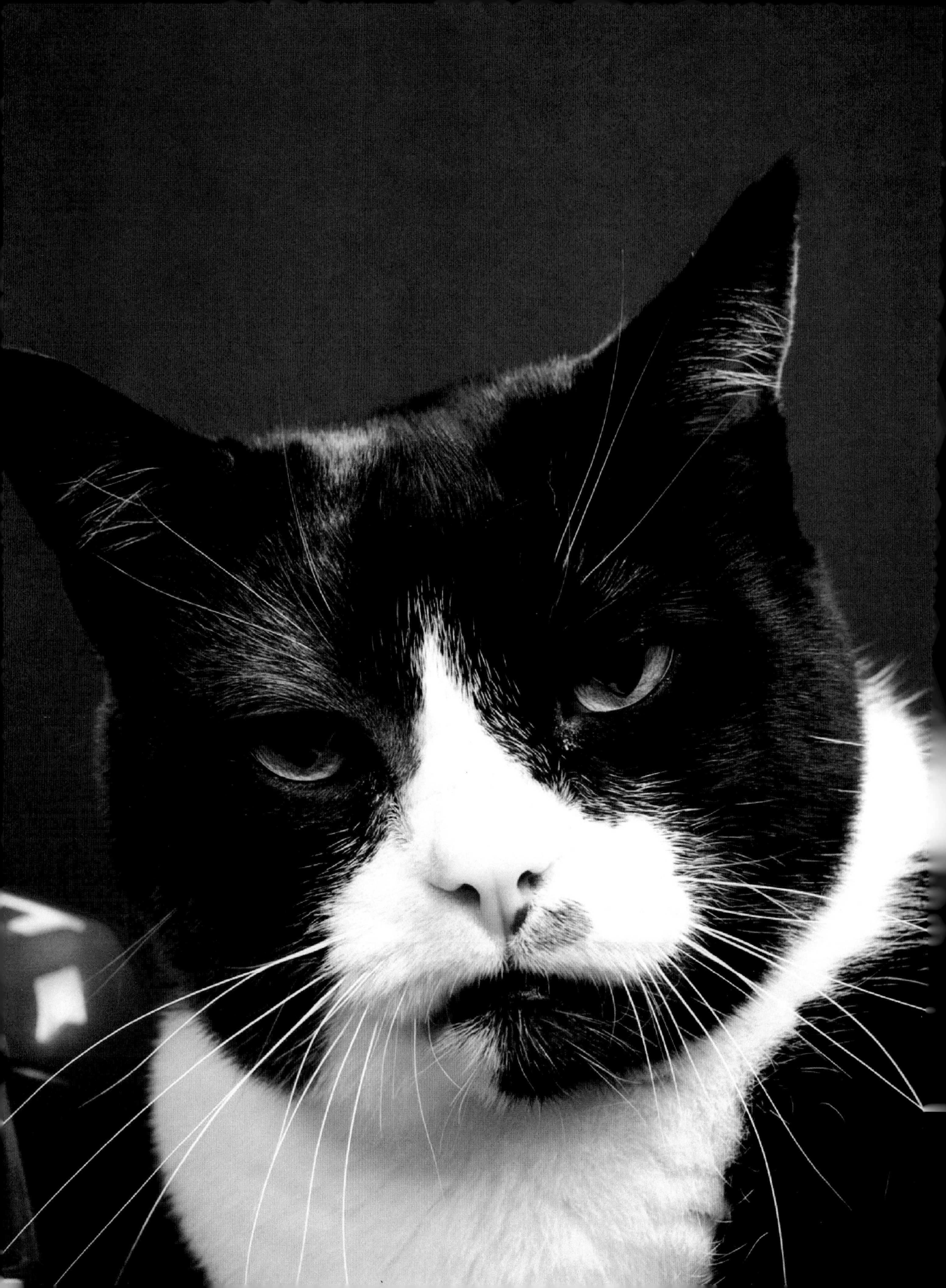

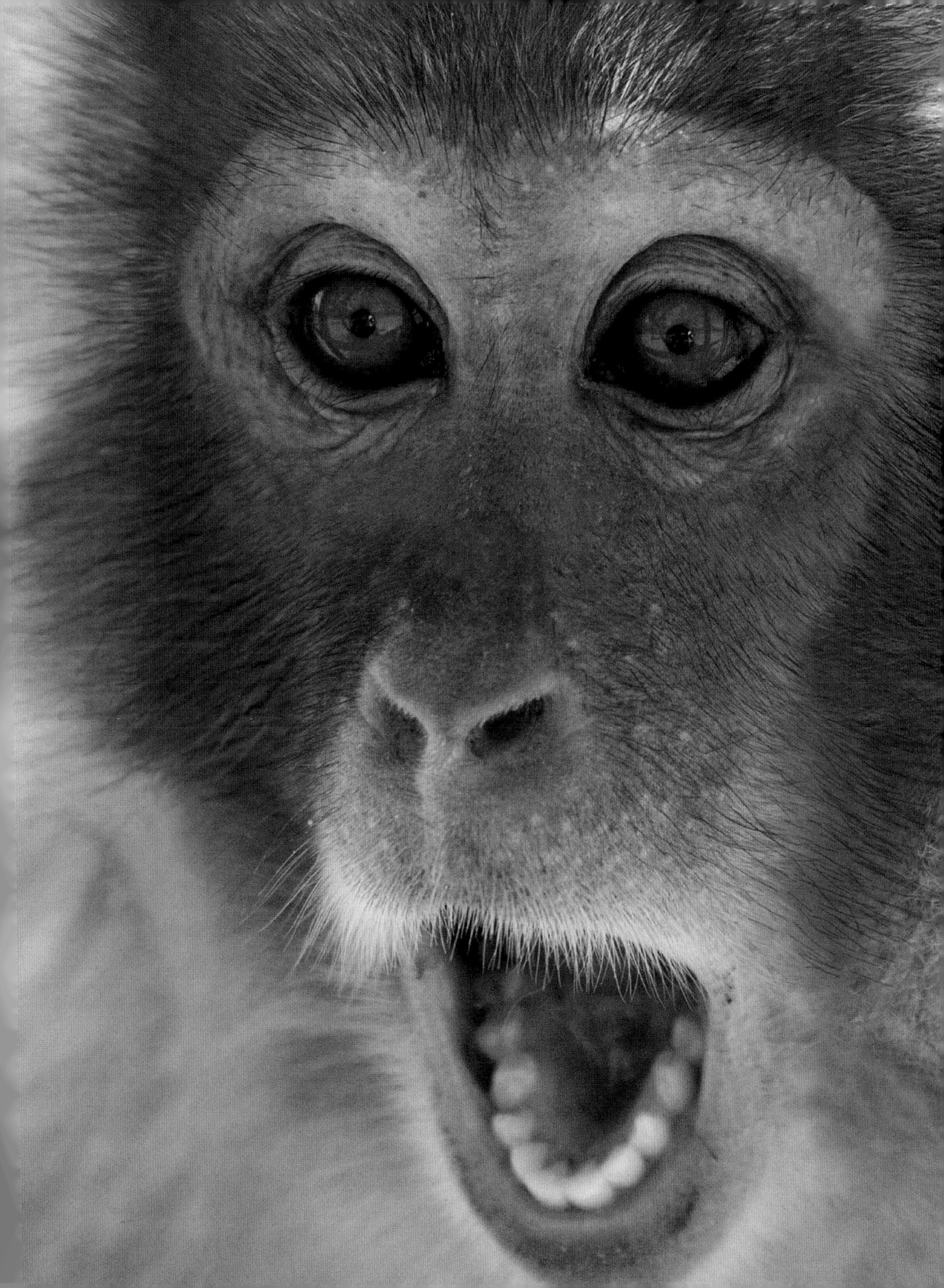

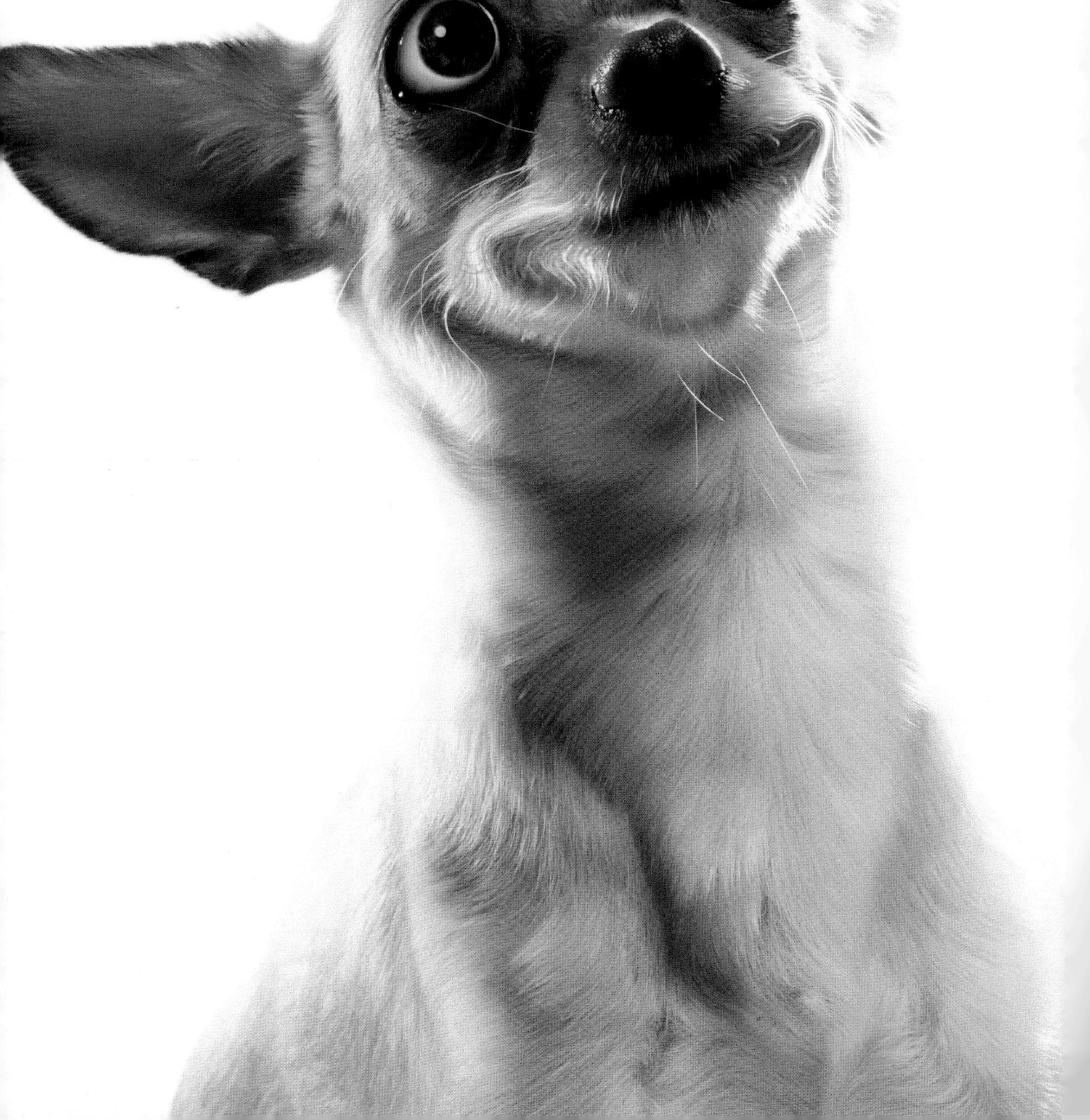

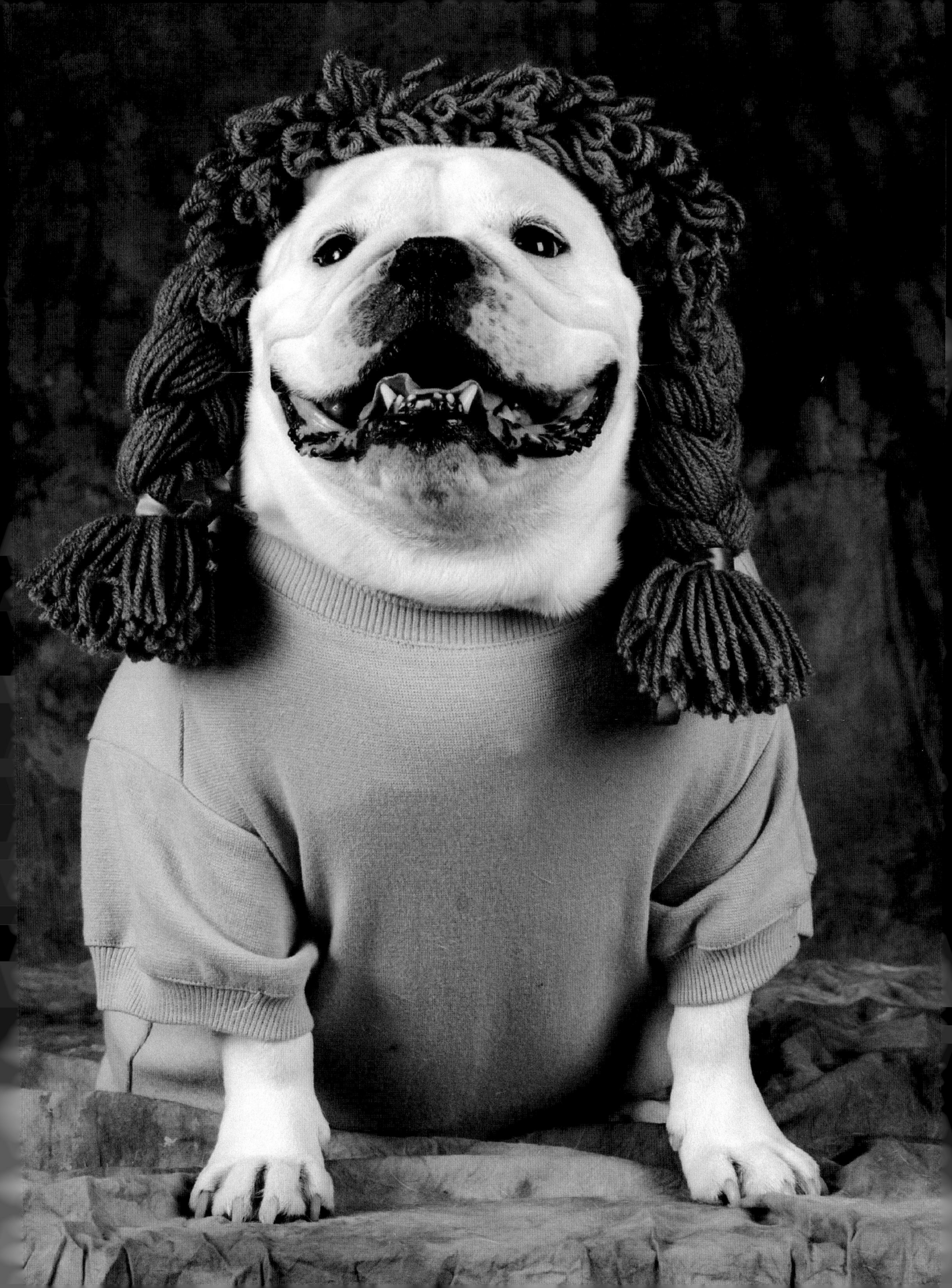

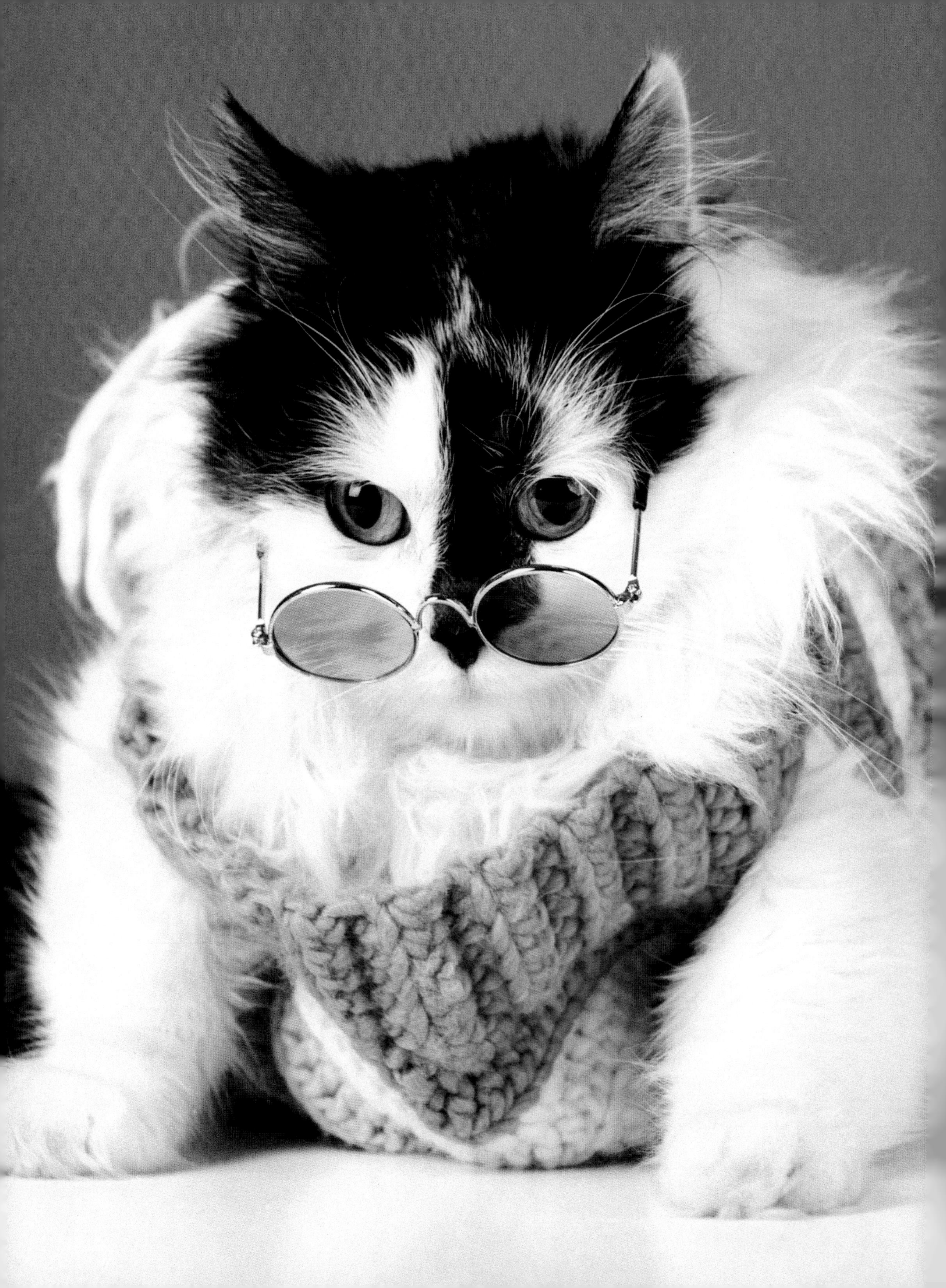

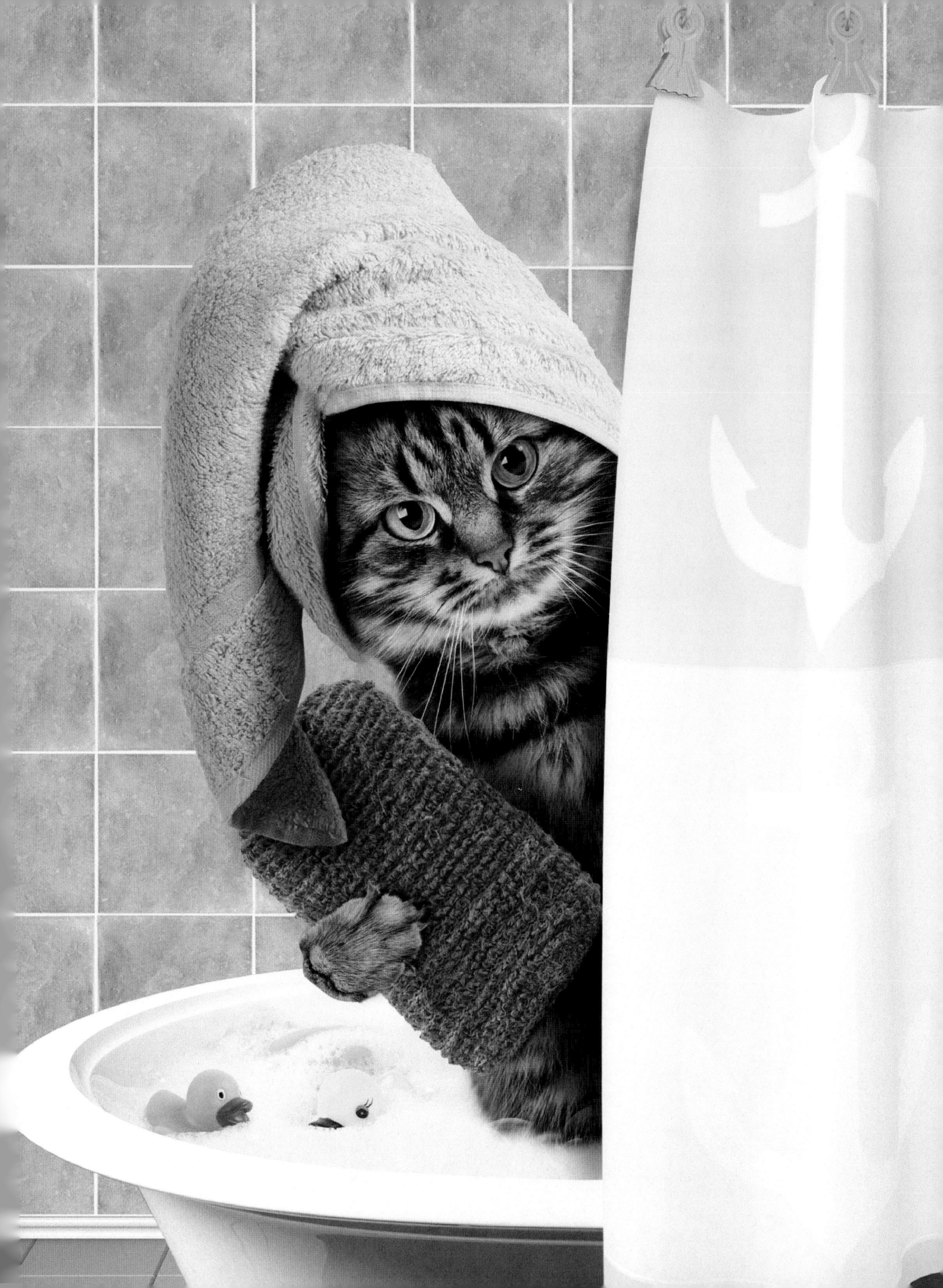

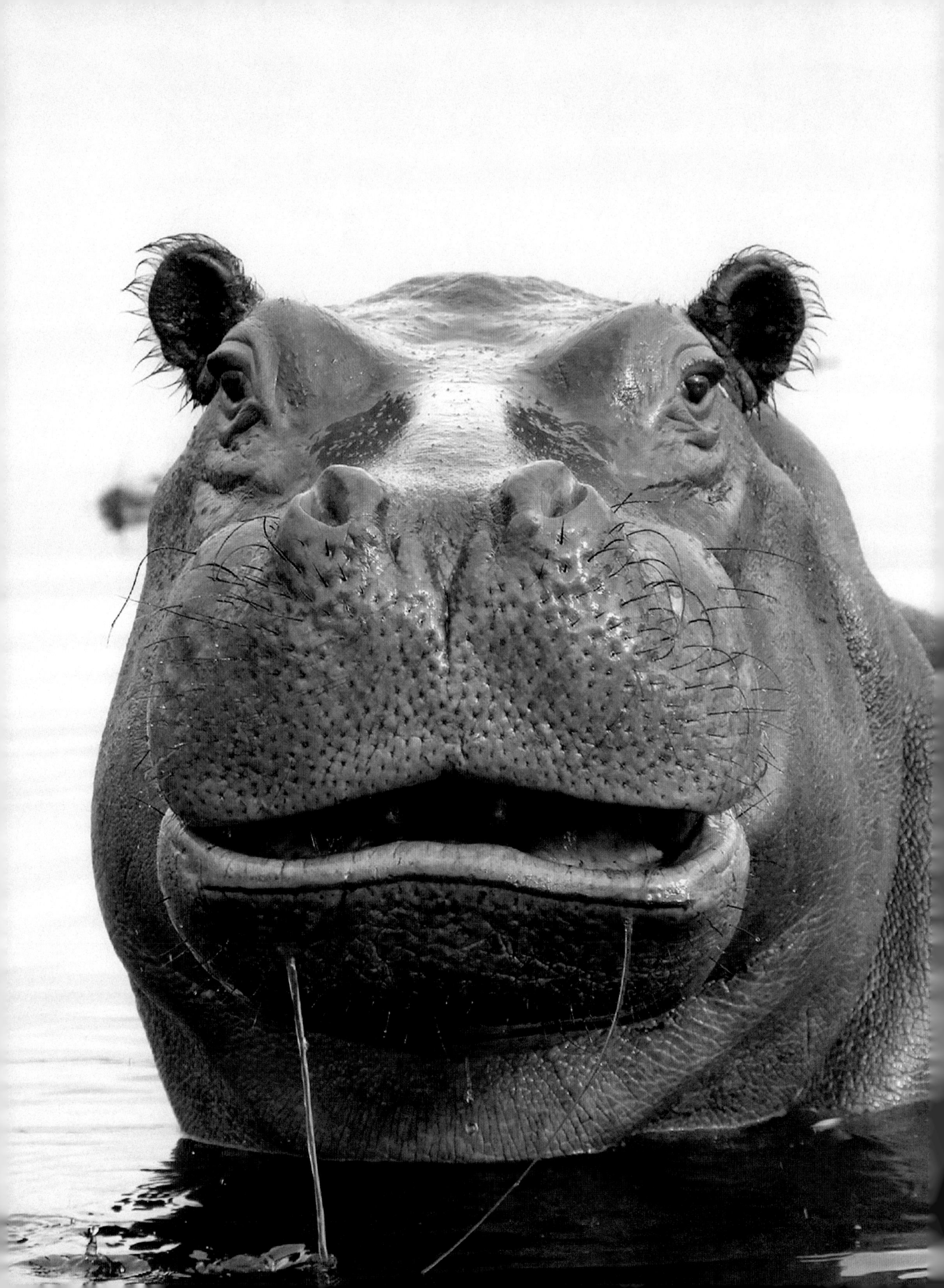

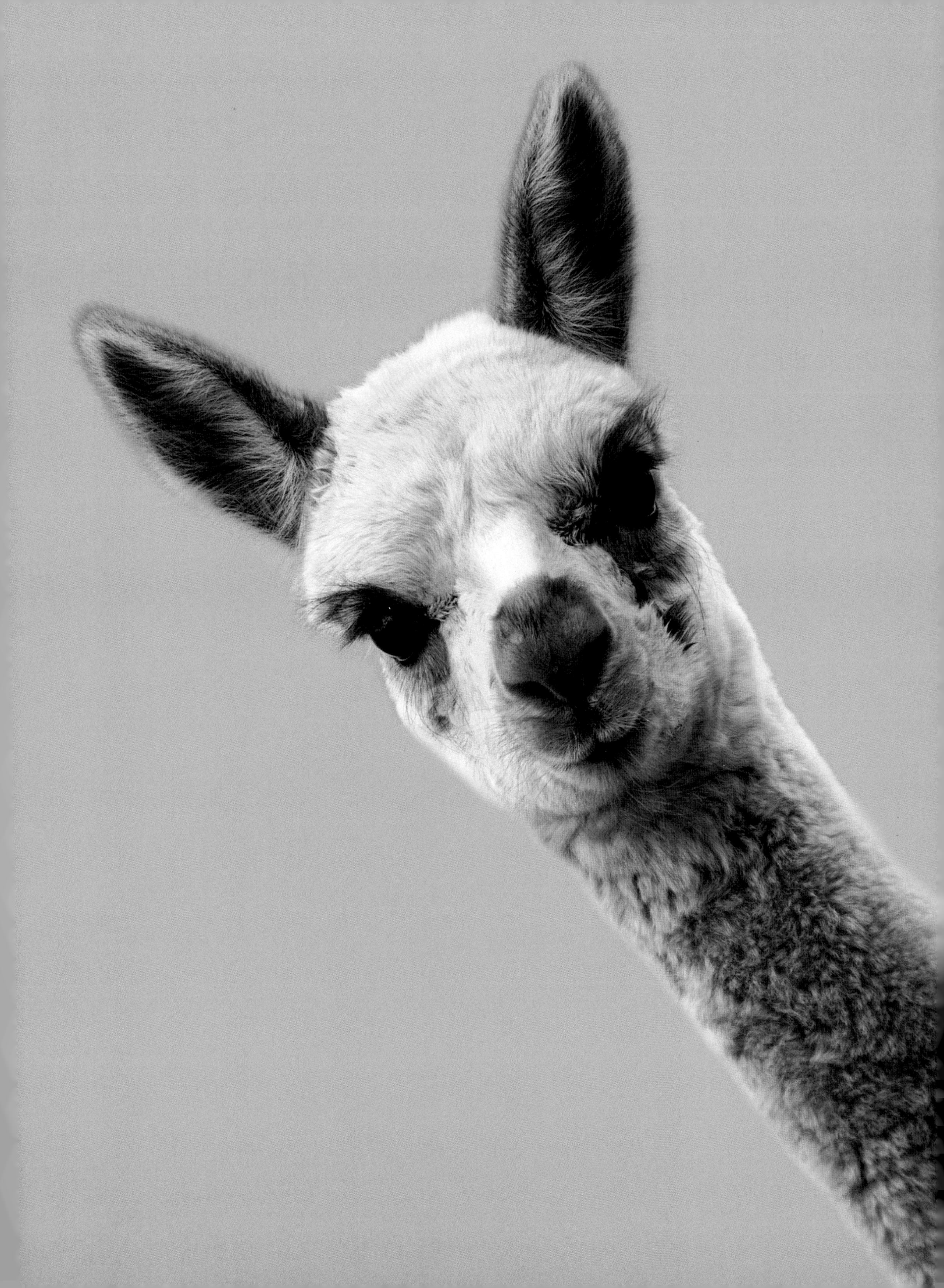

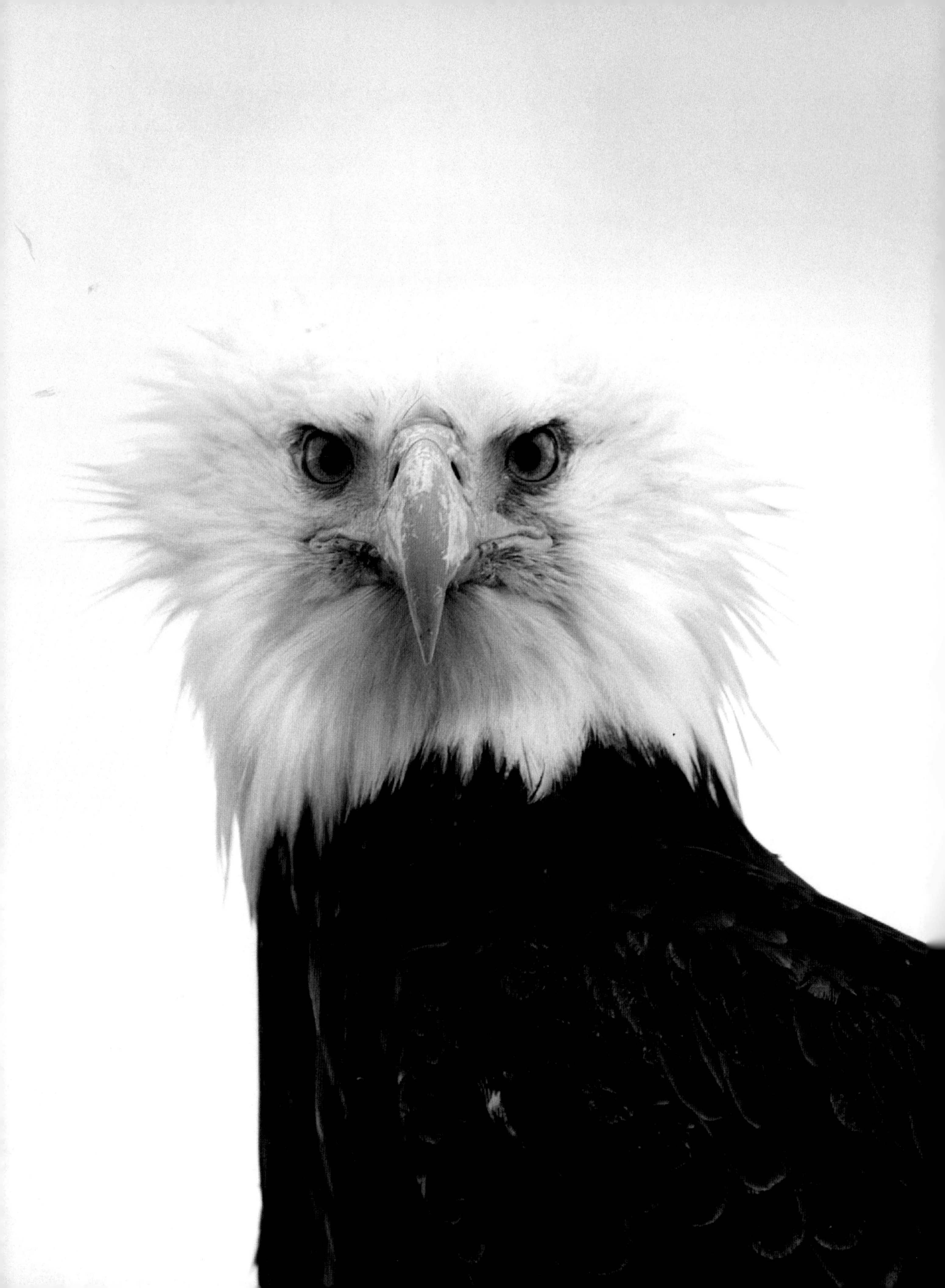

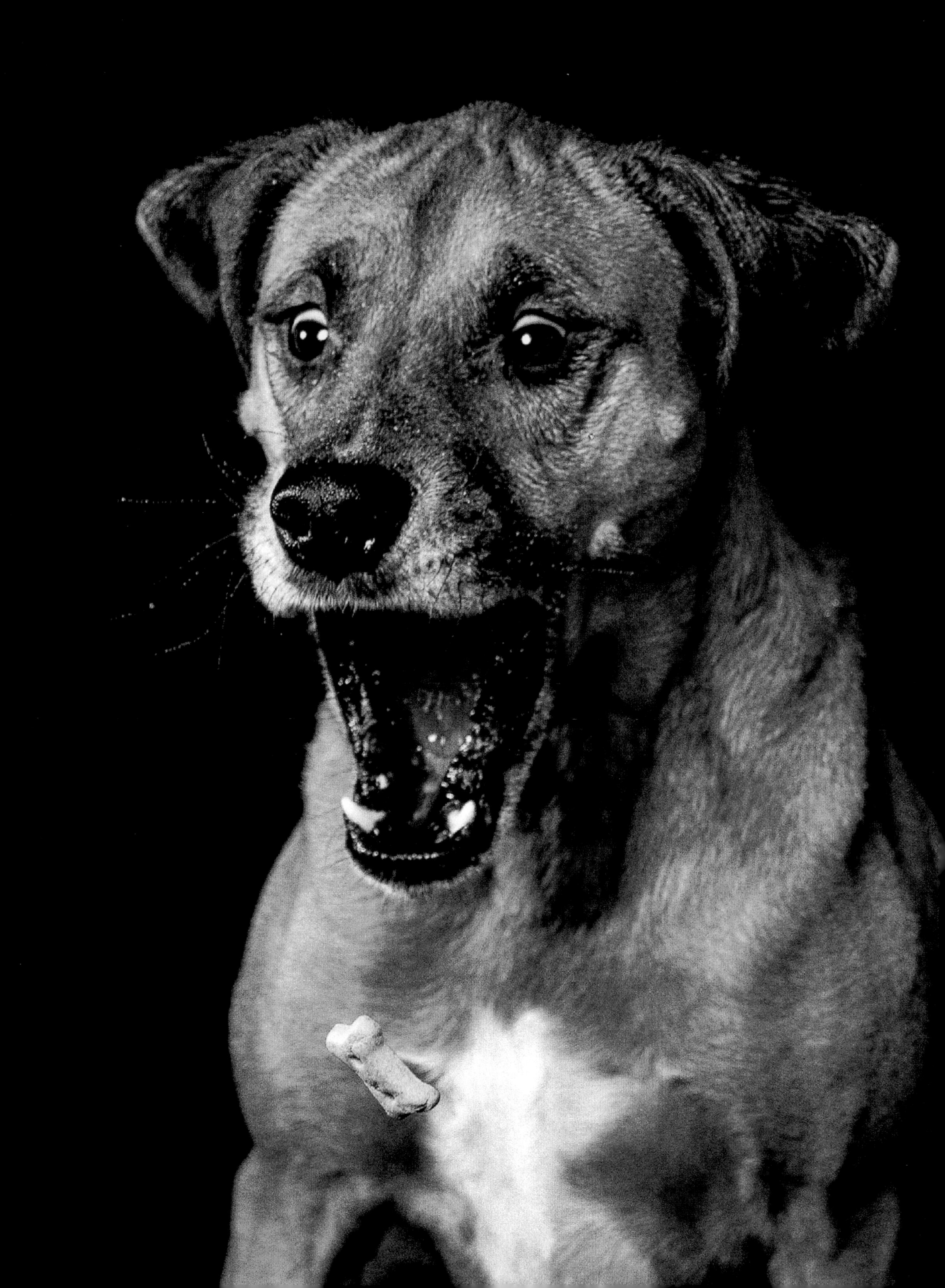

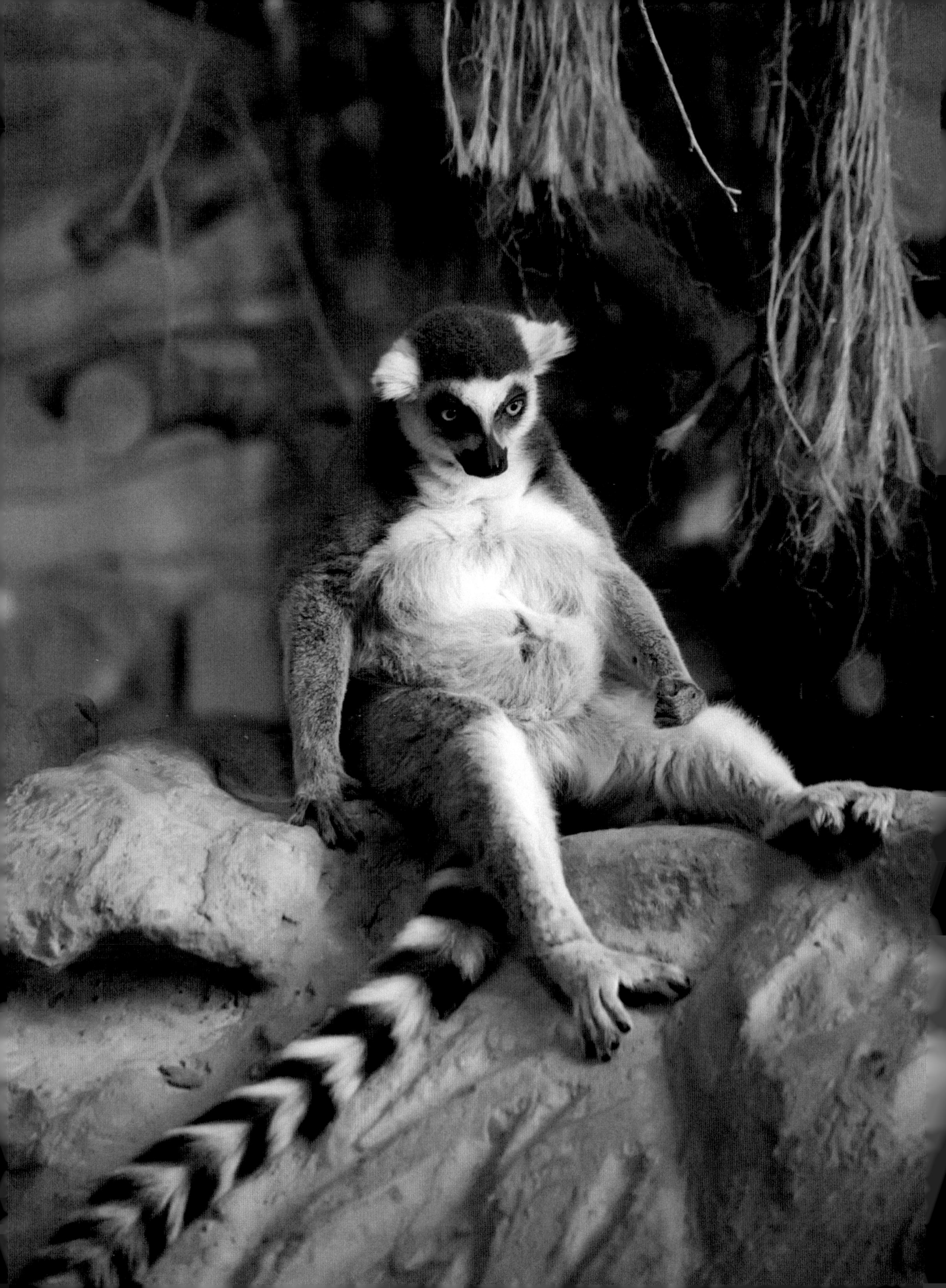

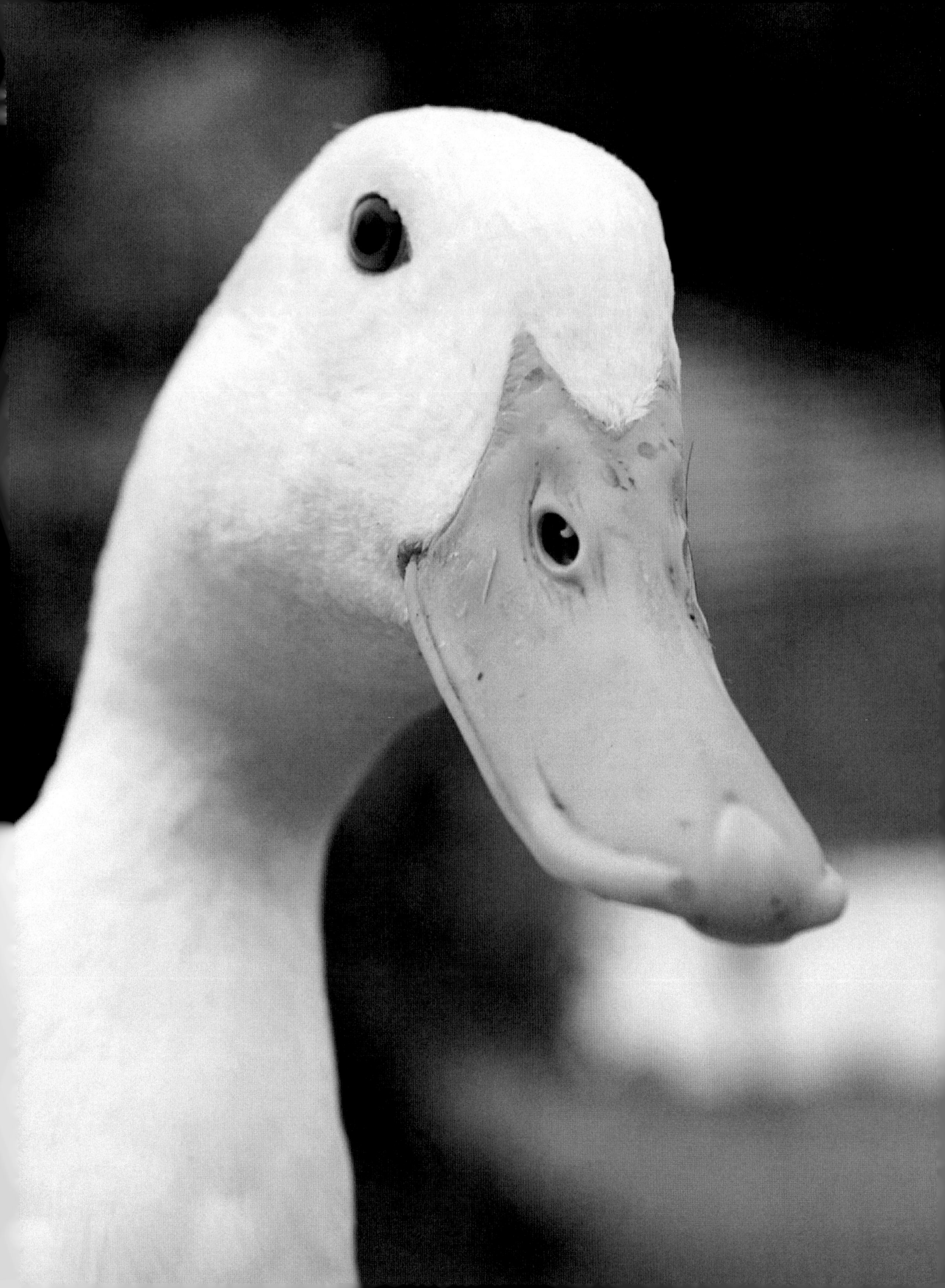

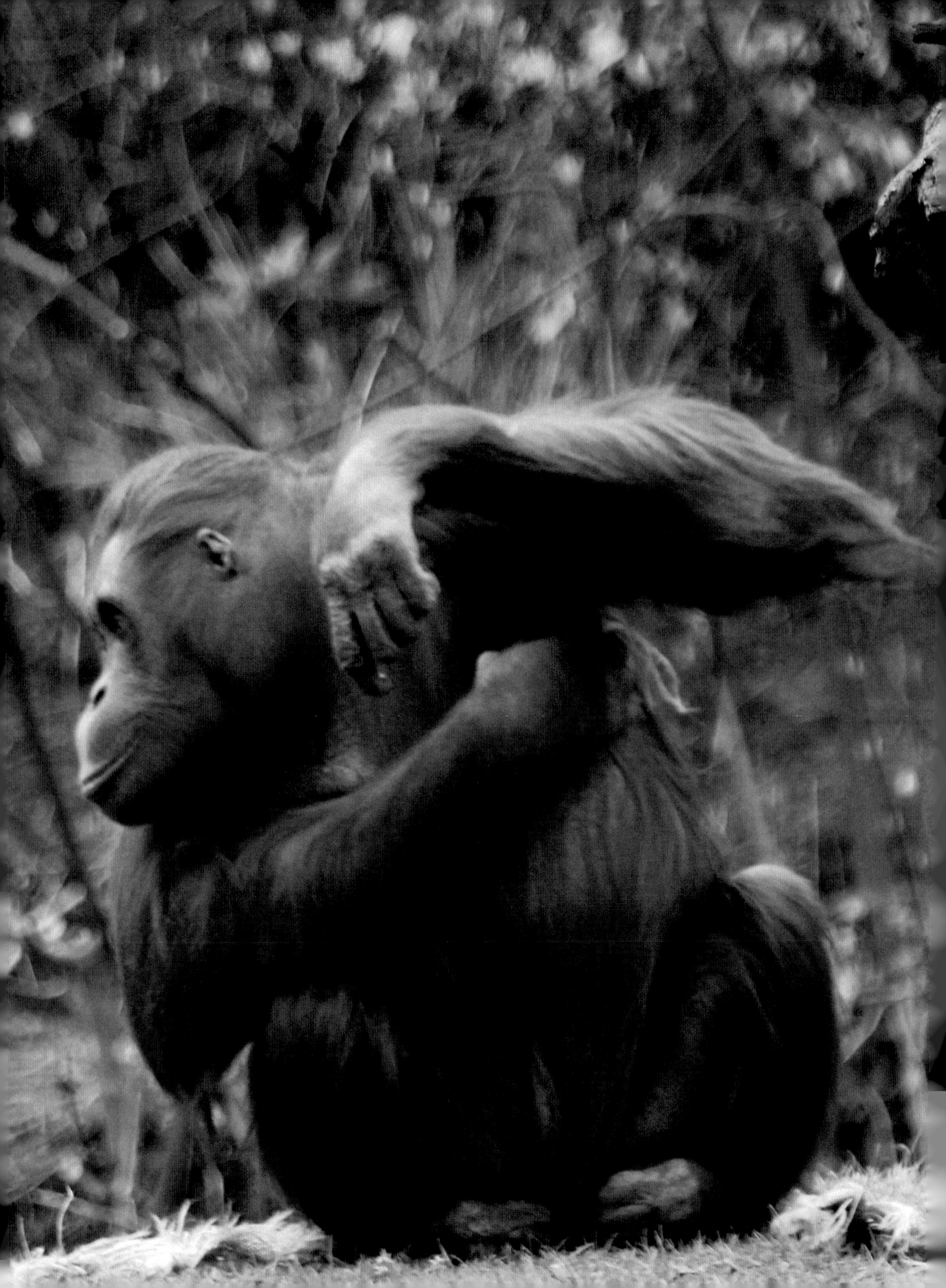

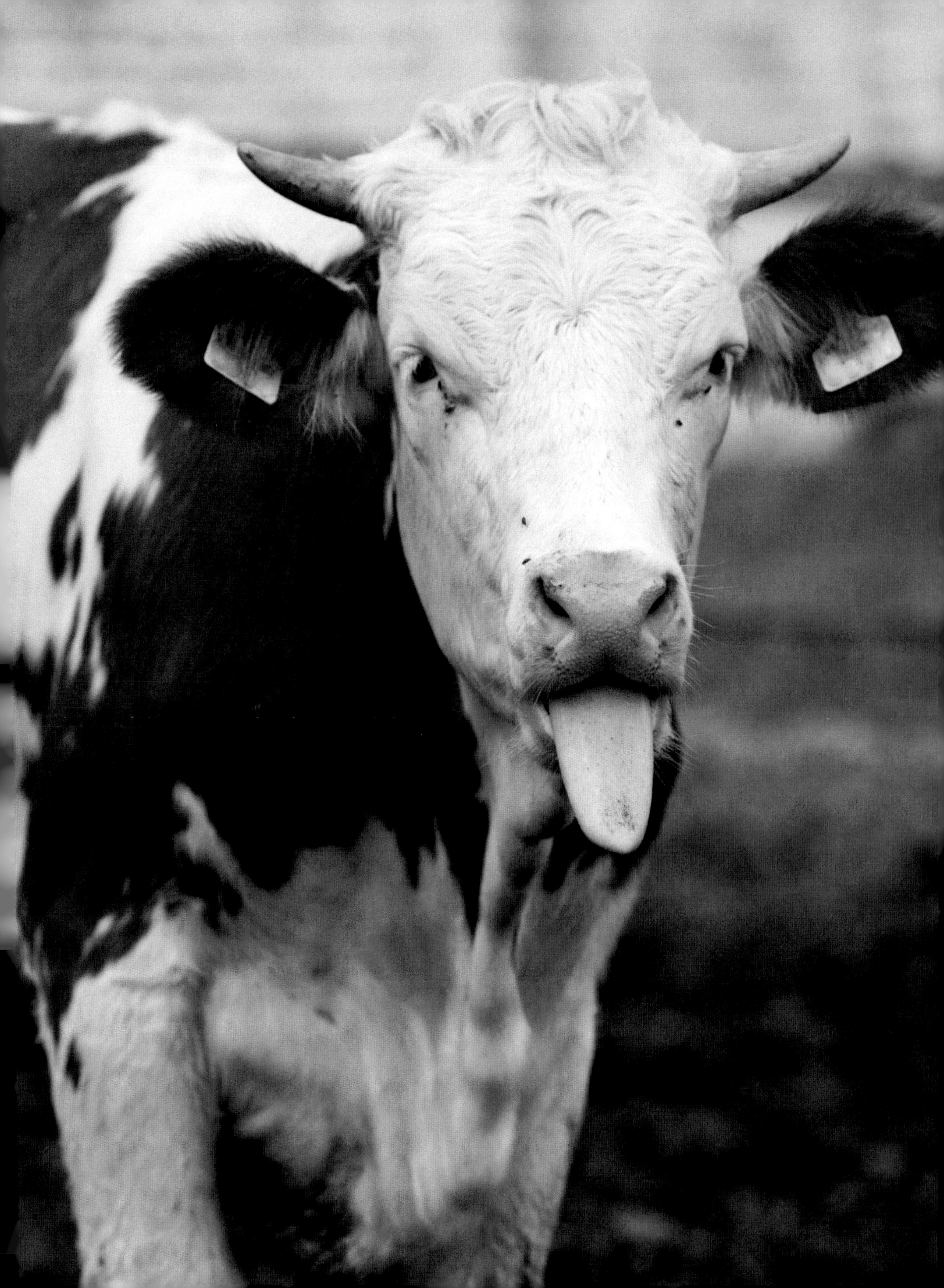

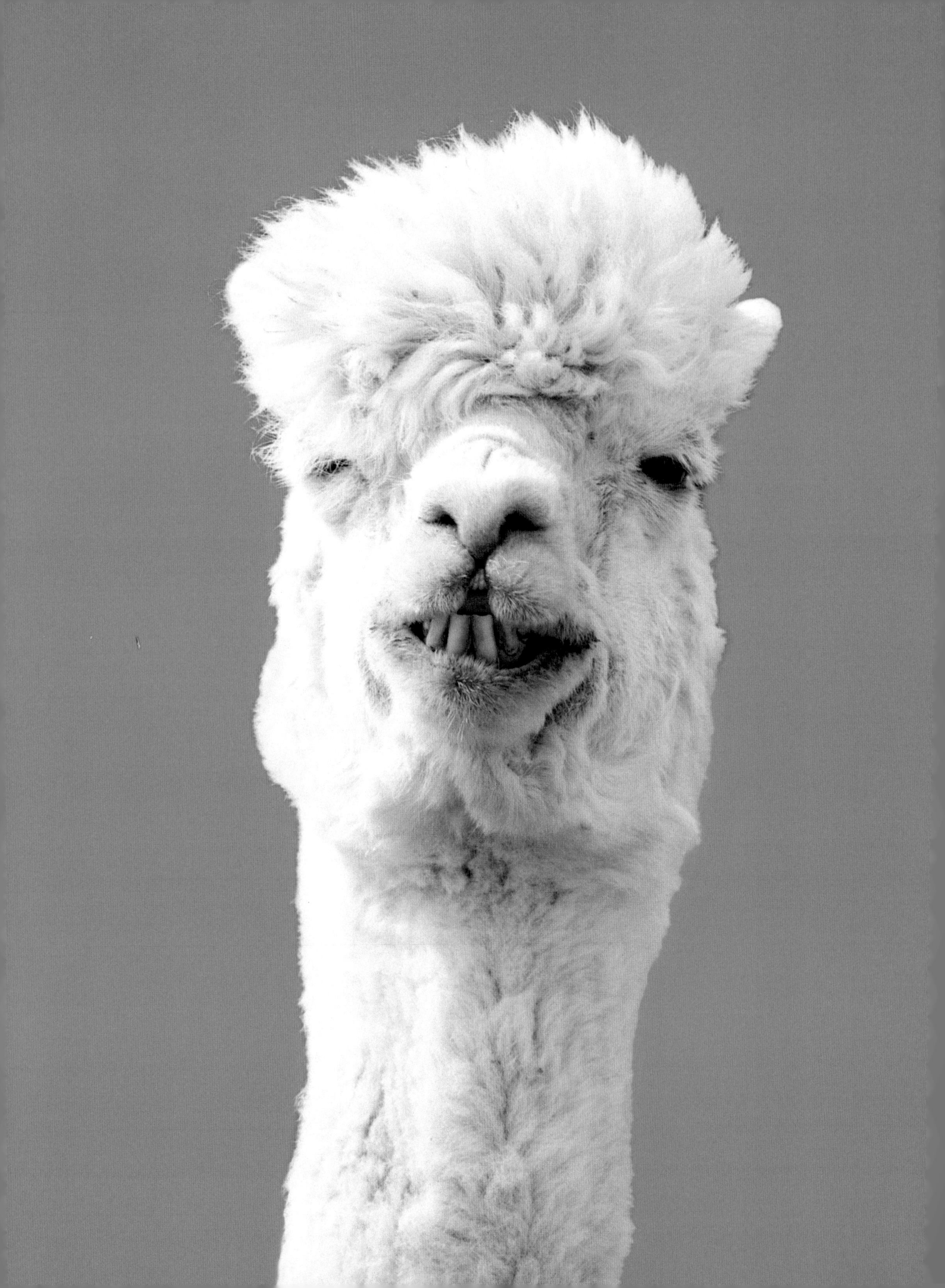

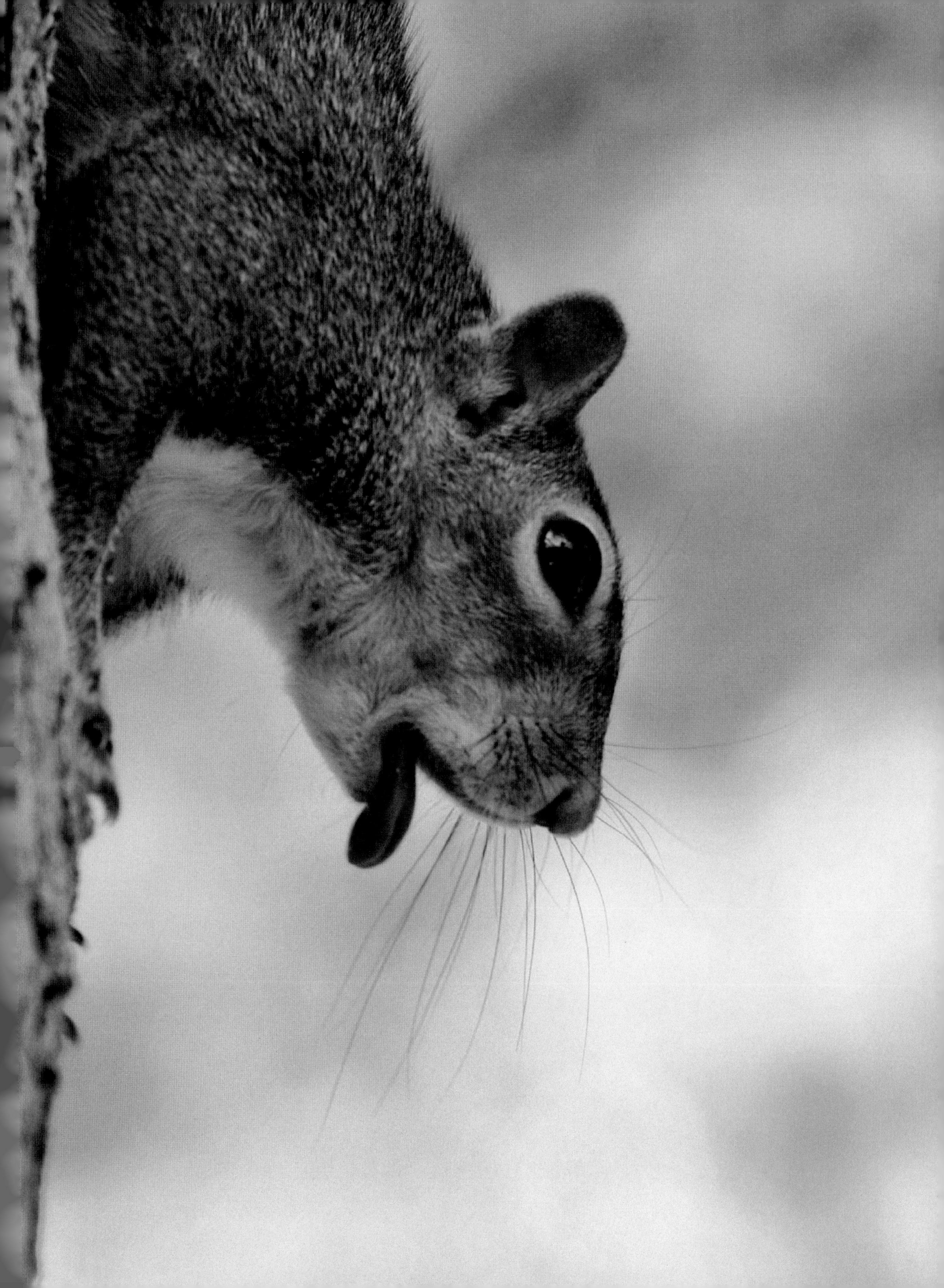

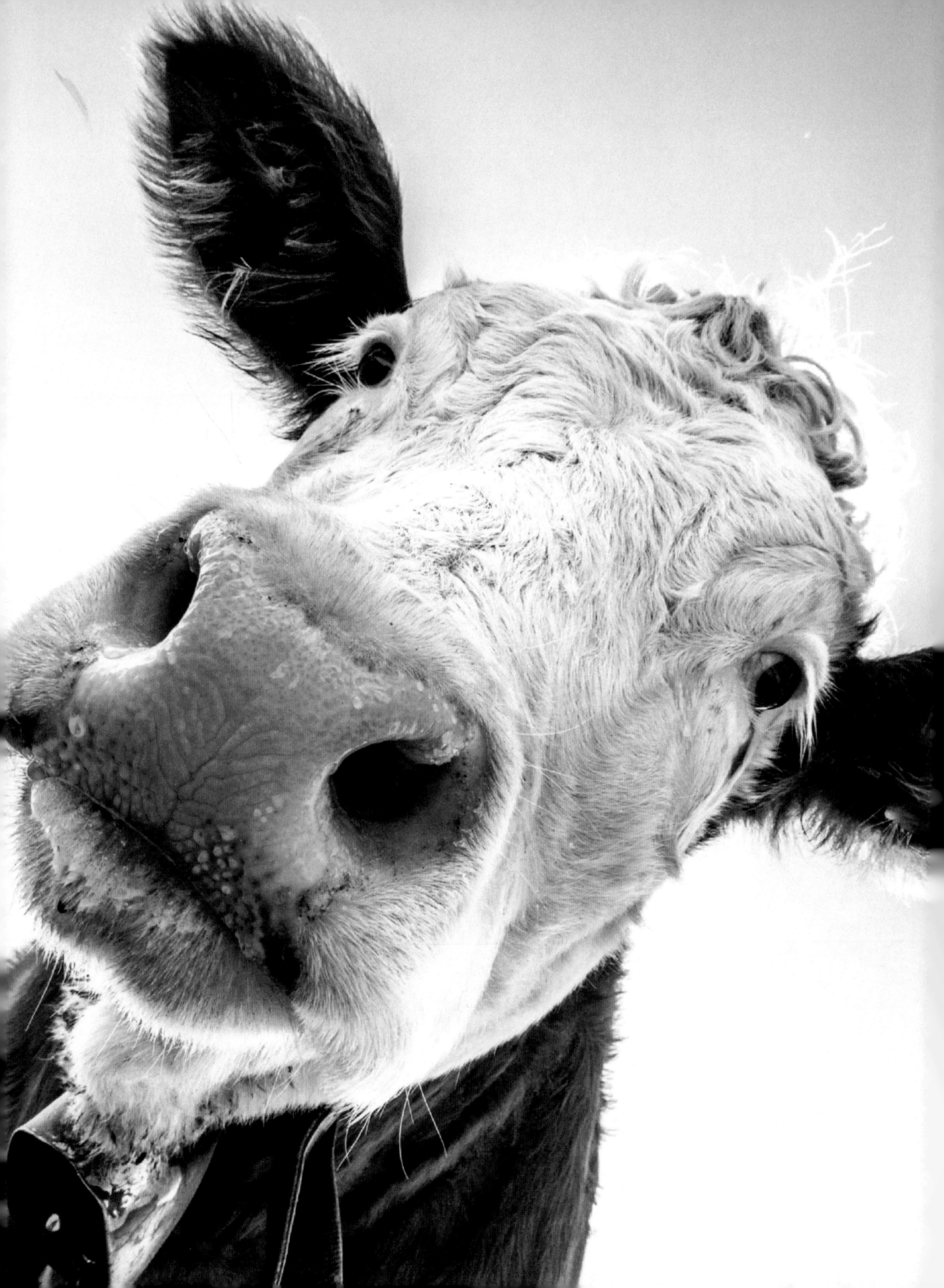

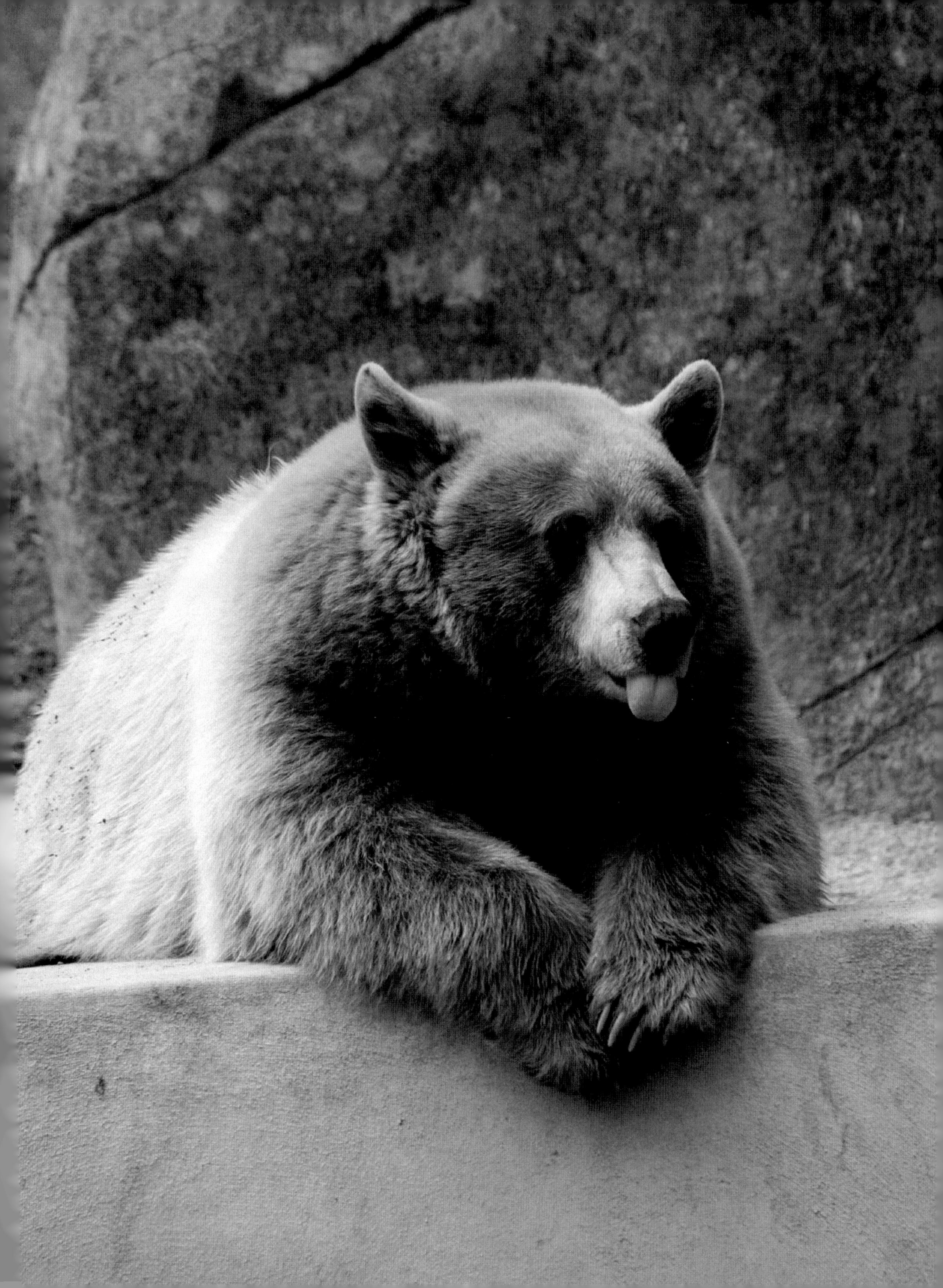

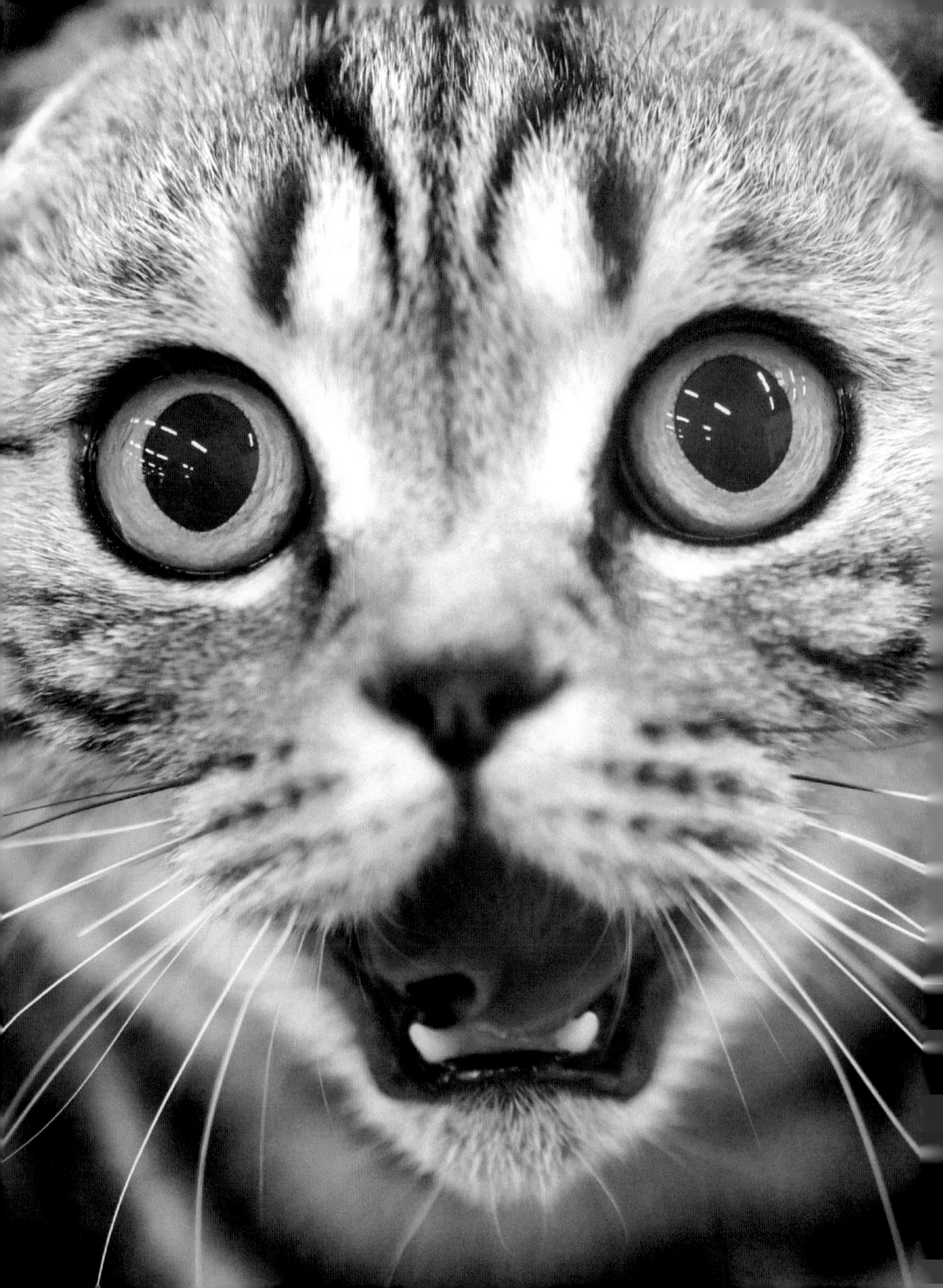

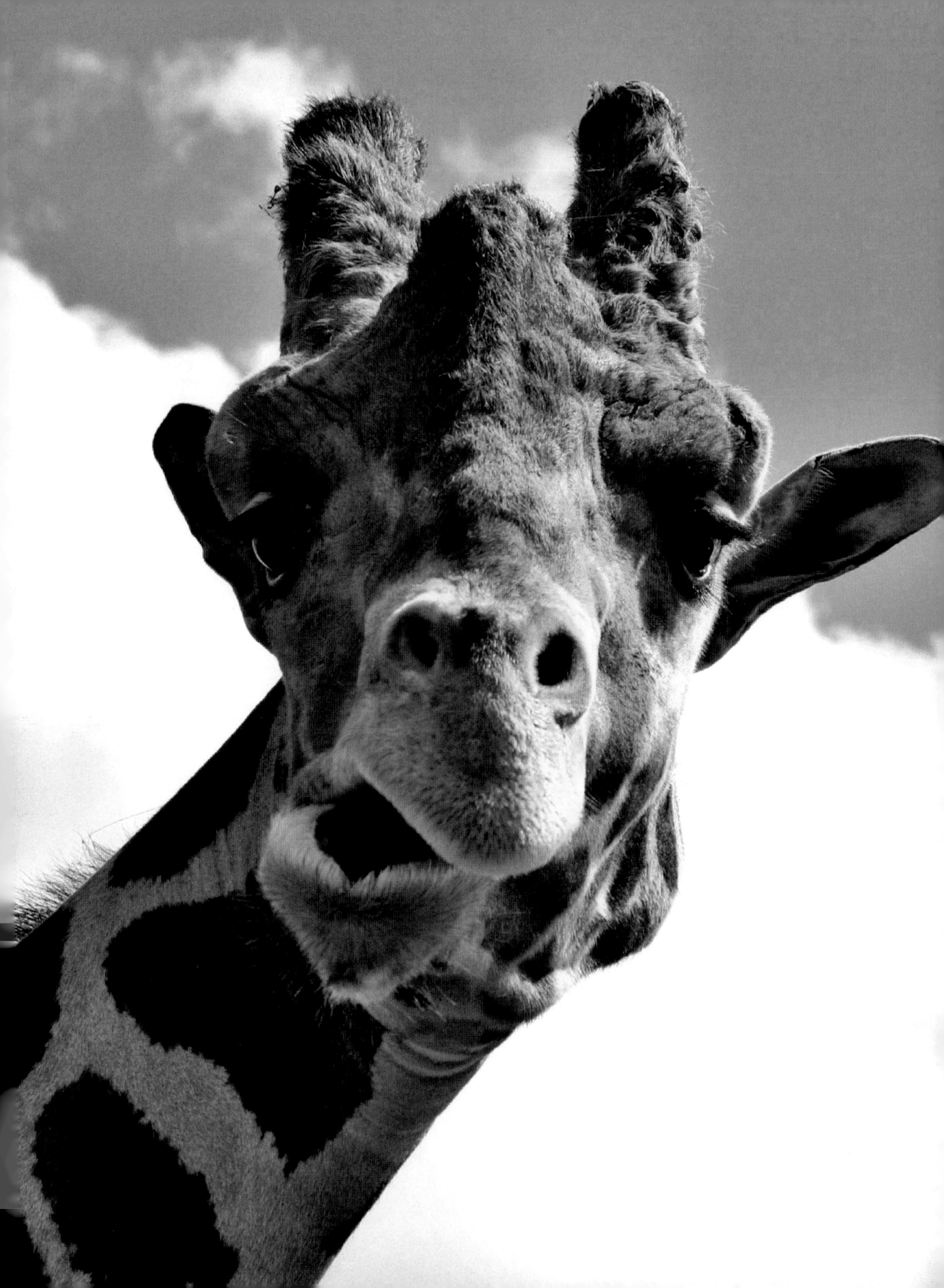

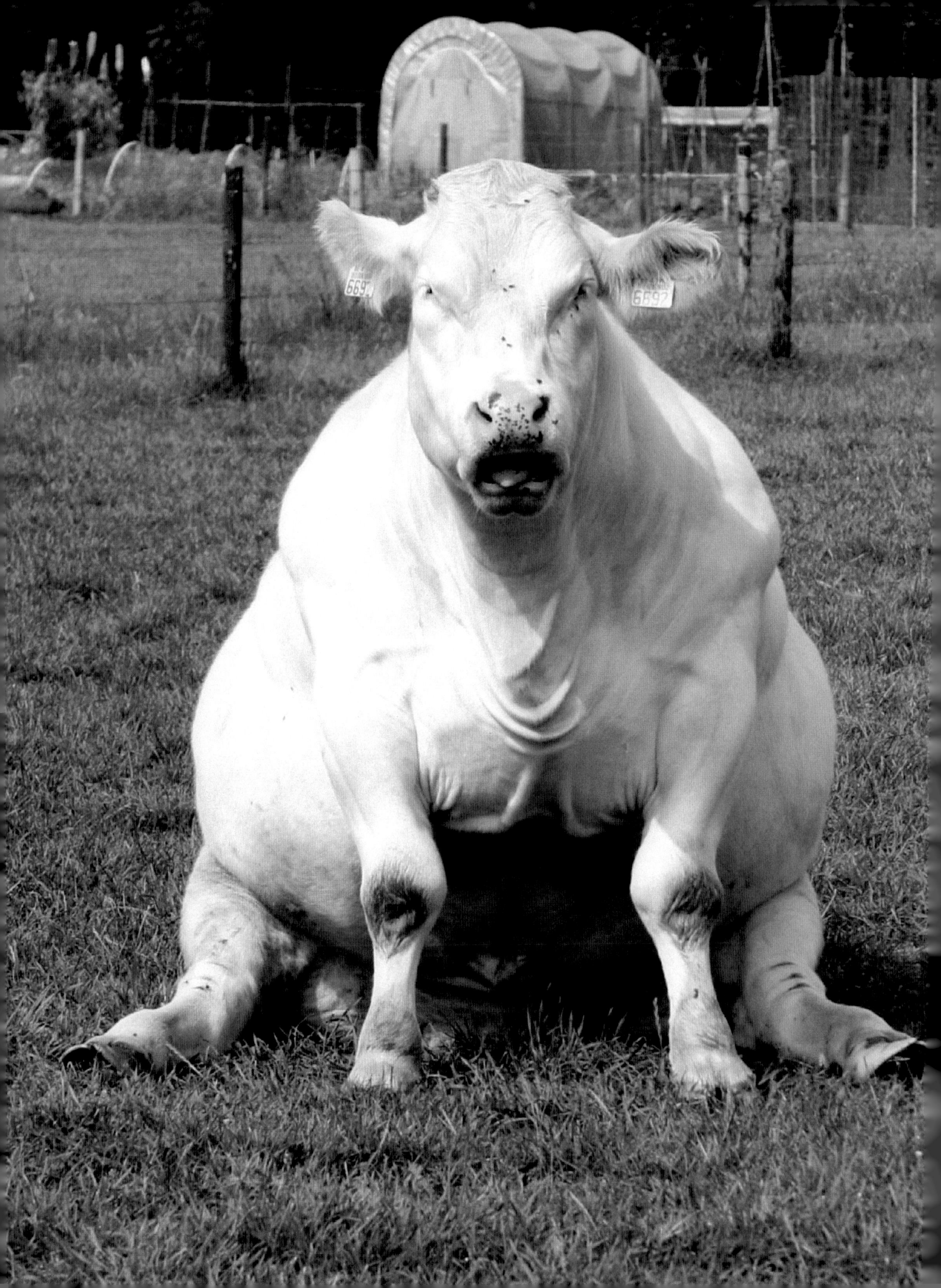
6697

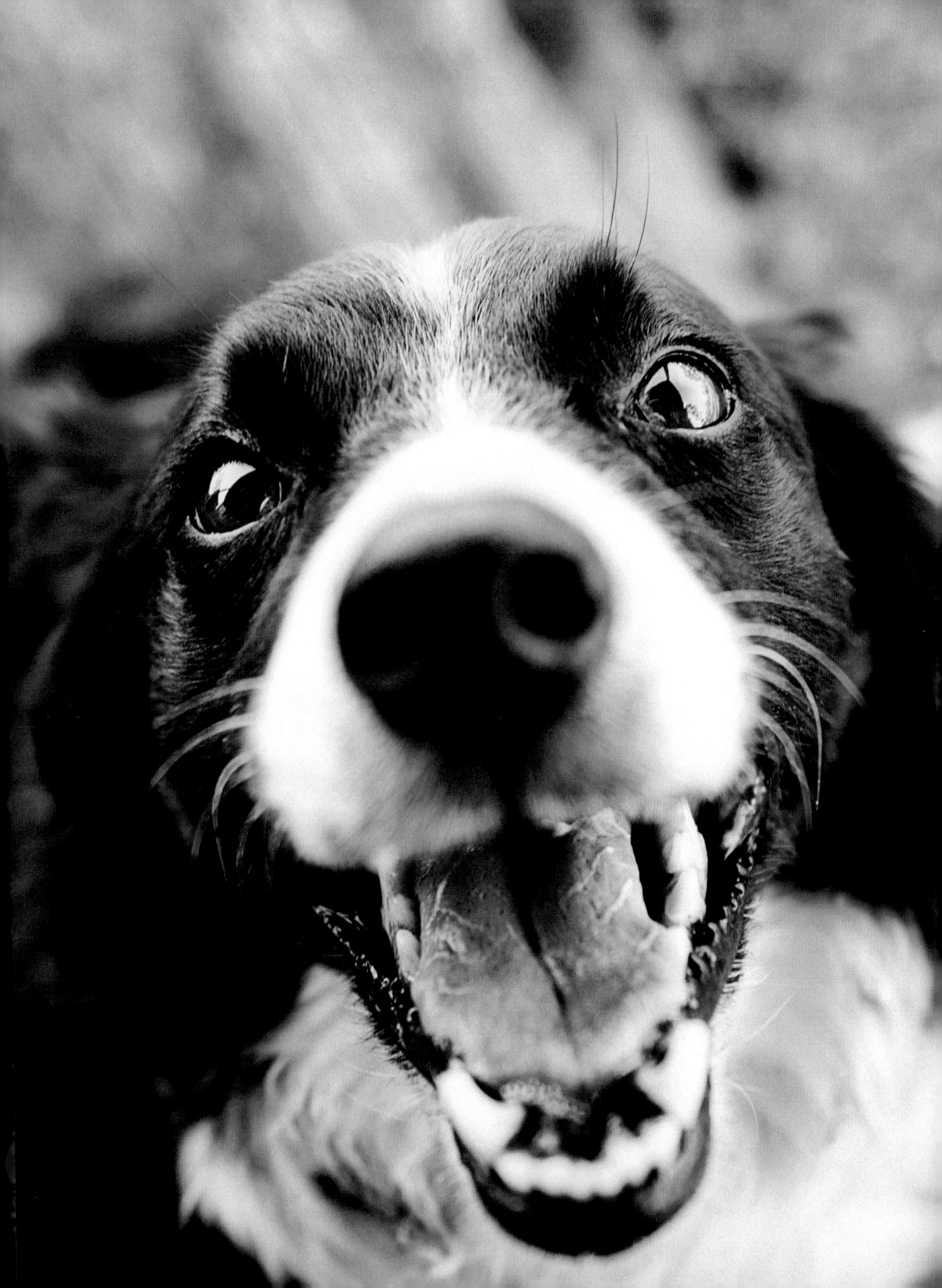

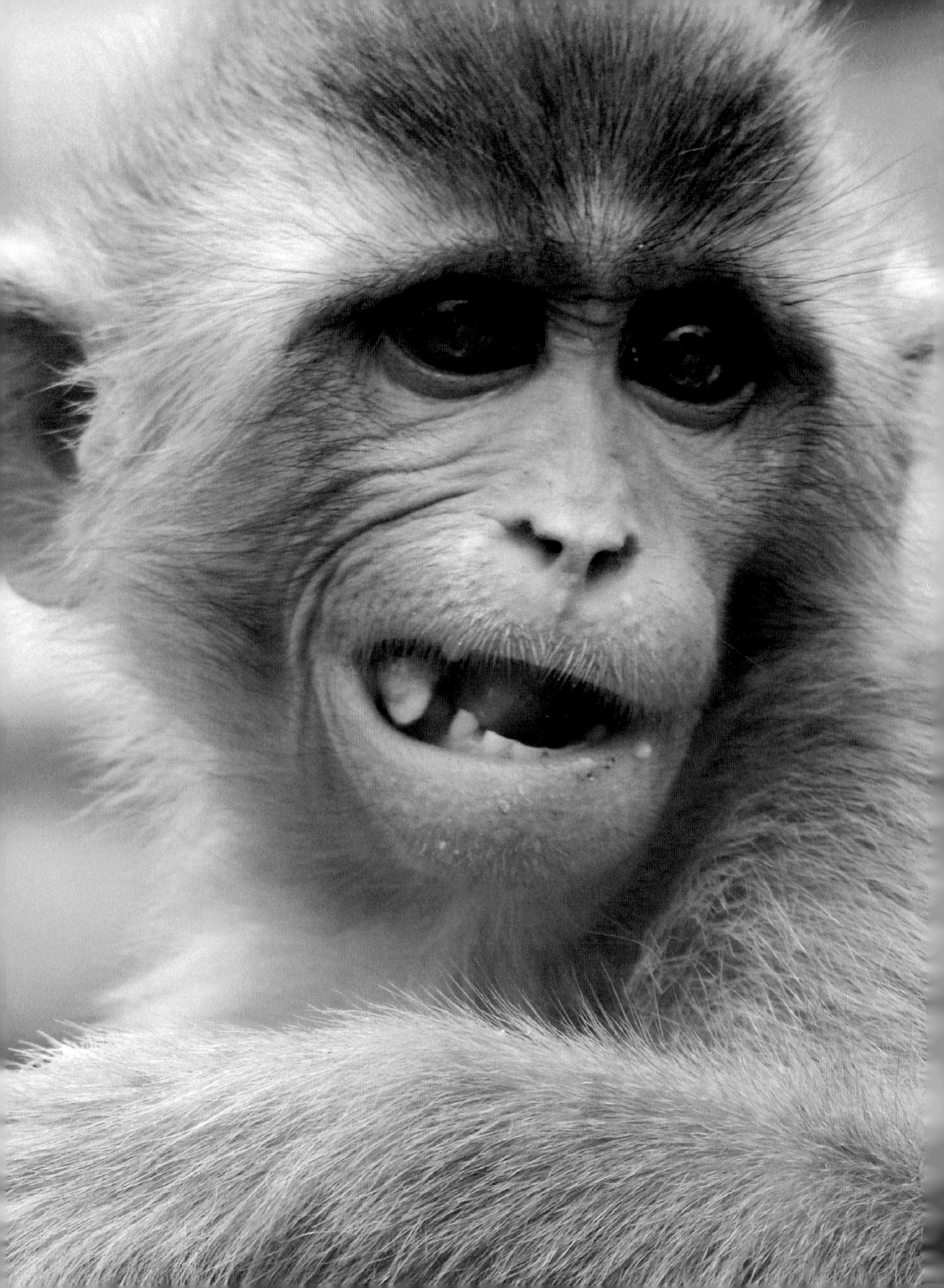

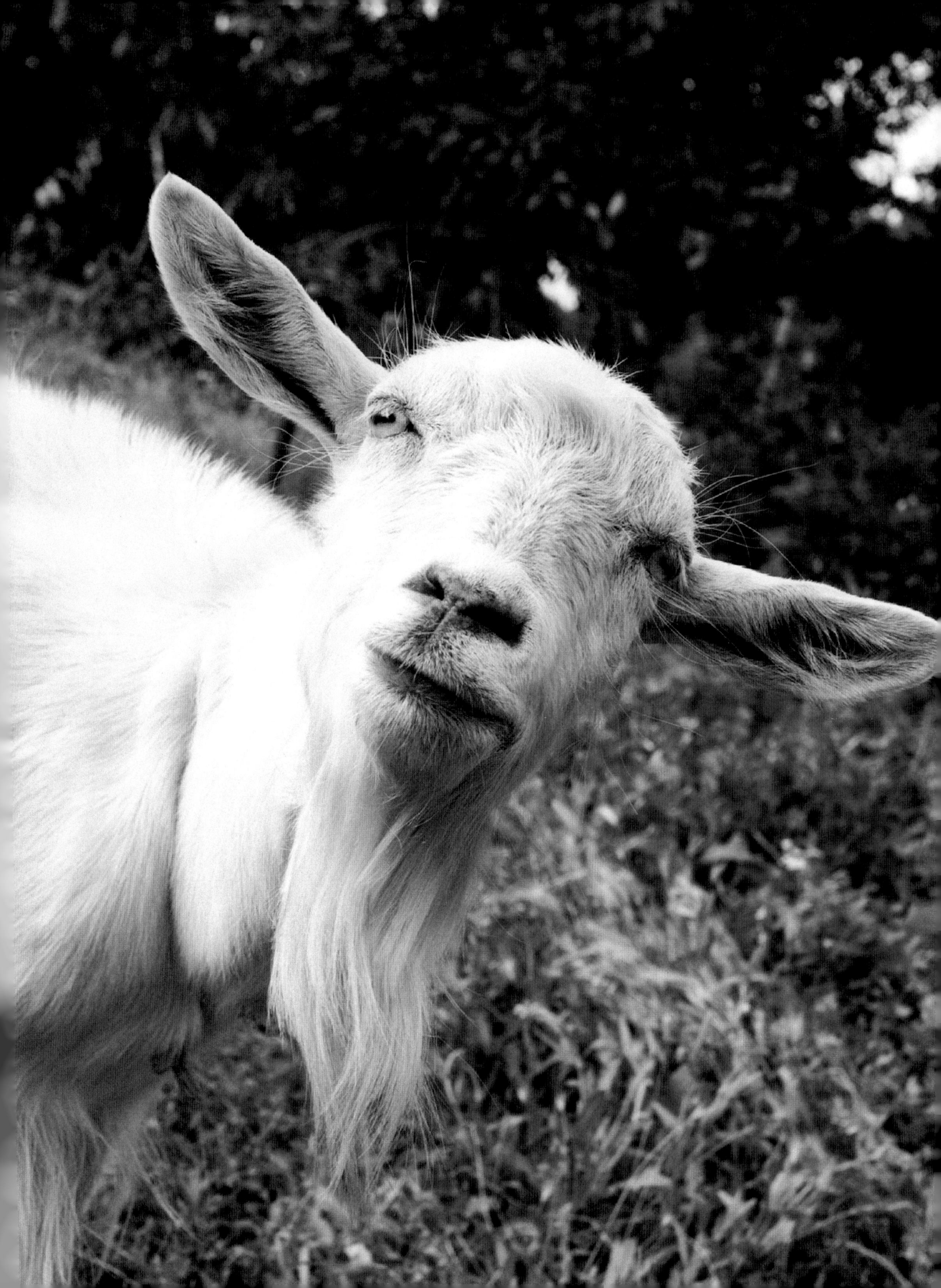

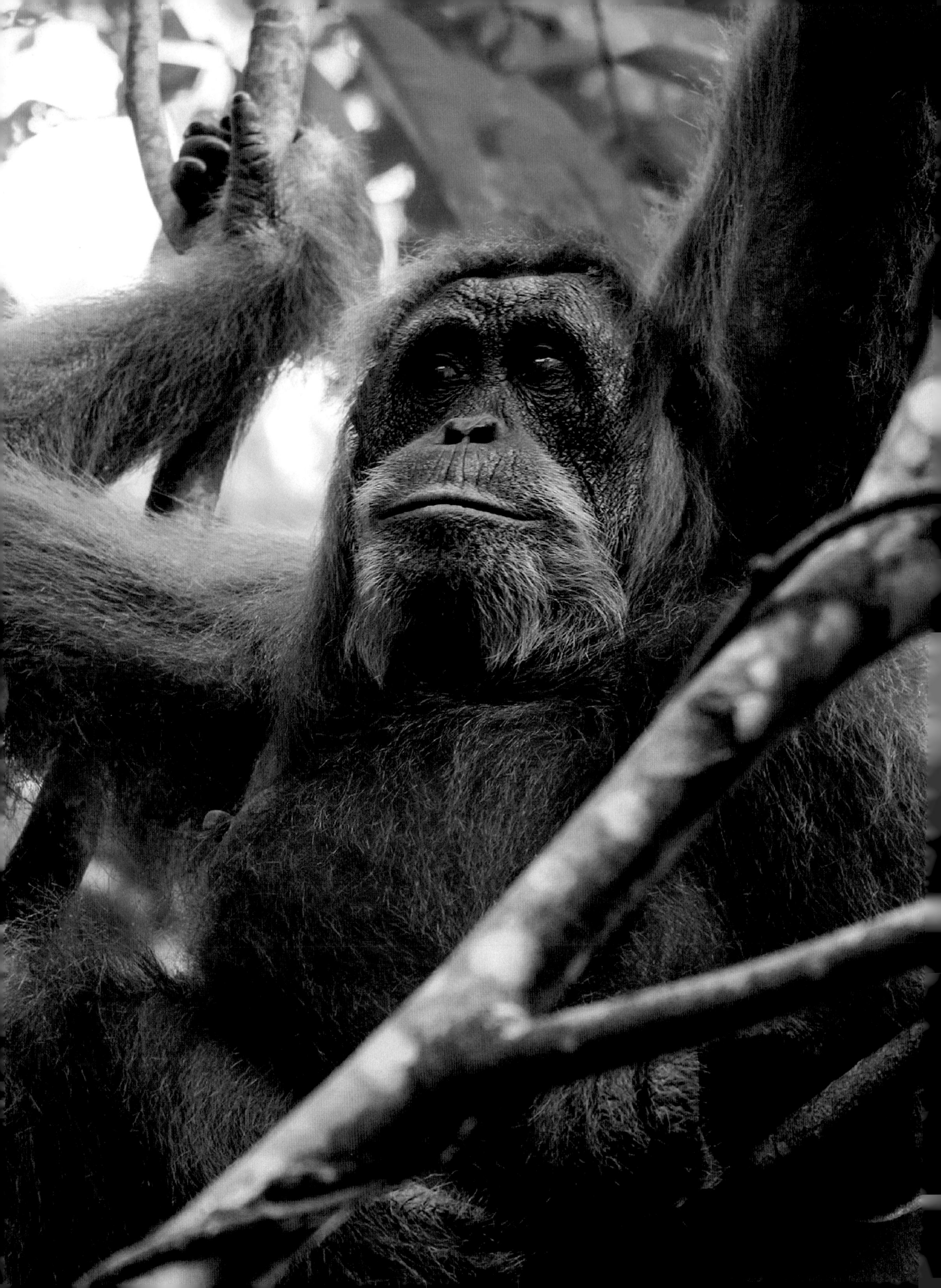

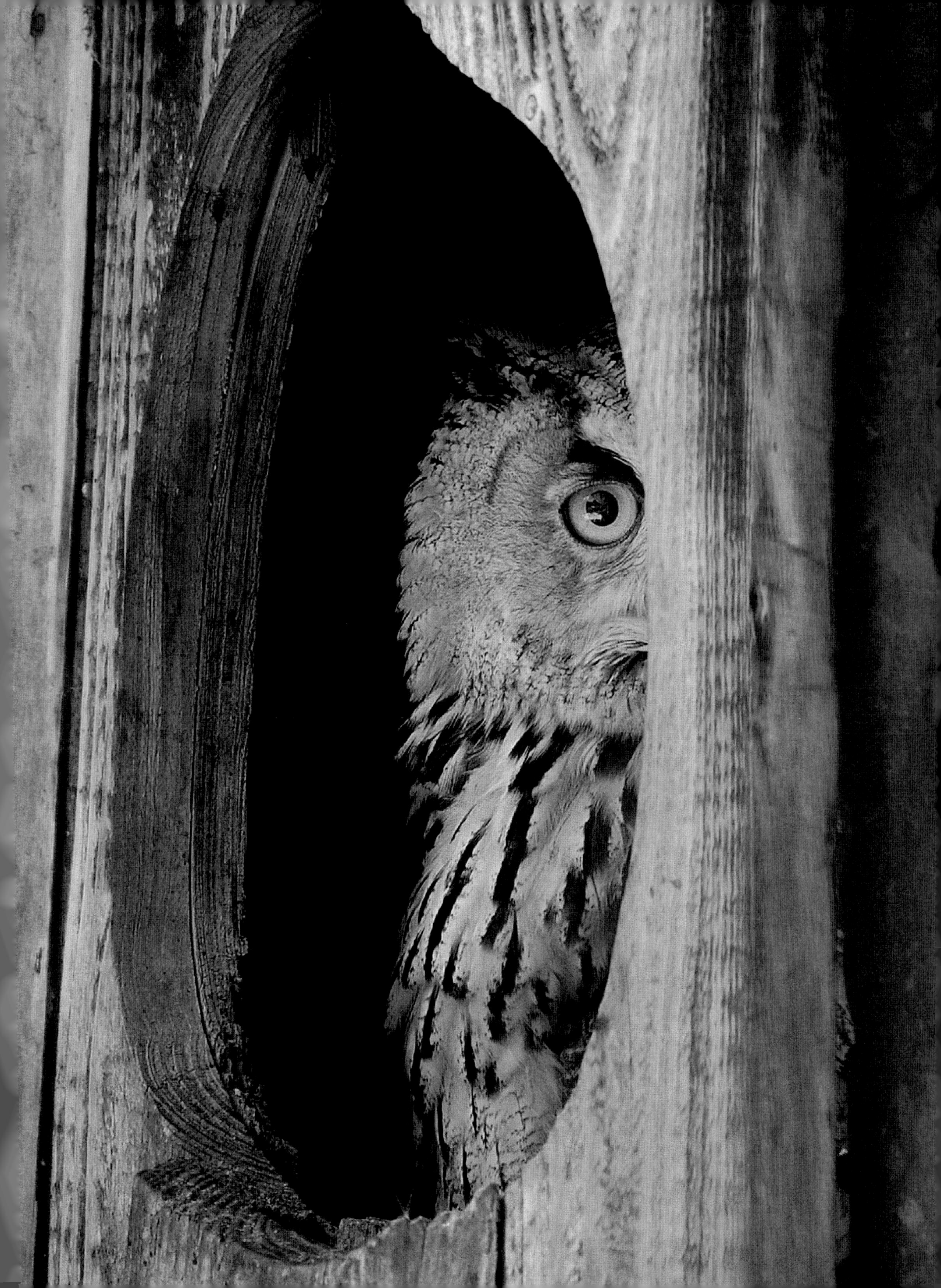

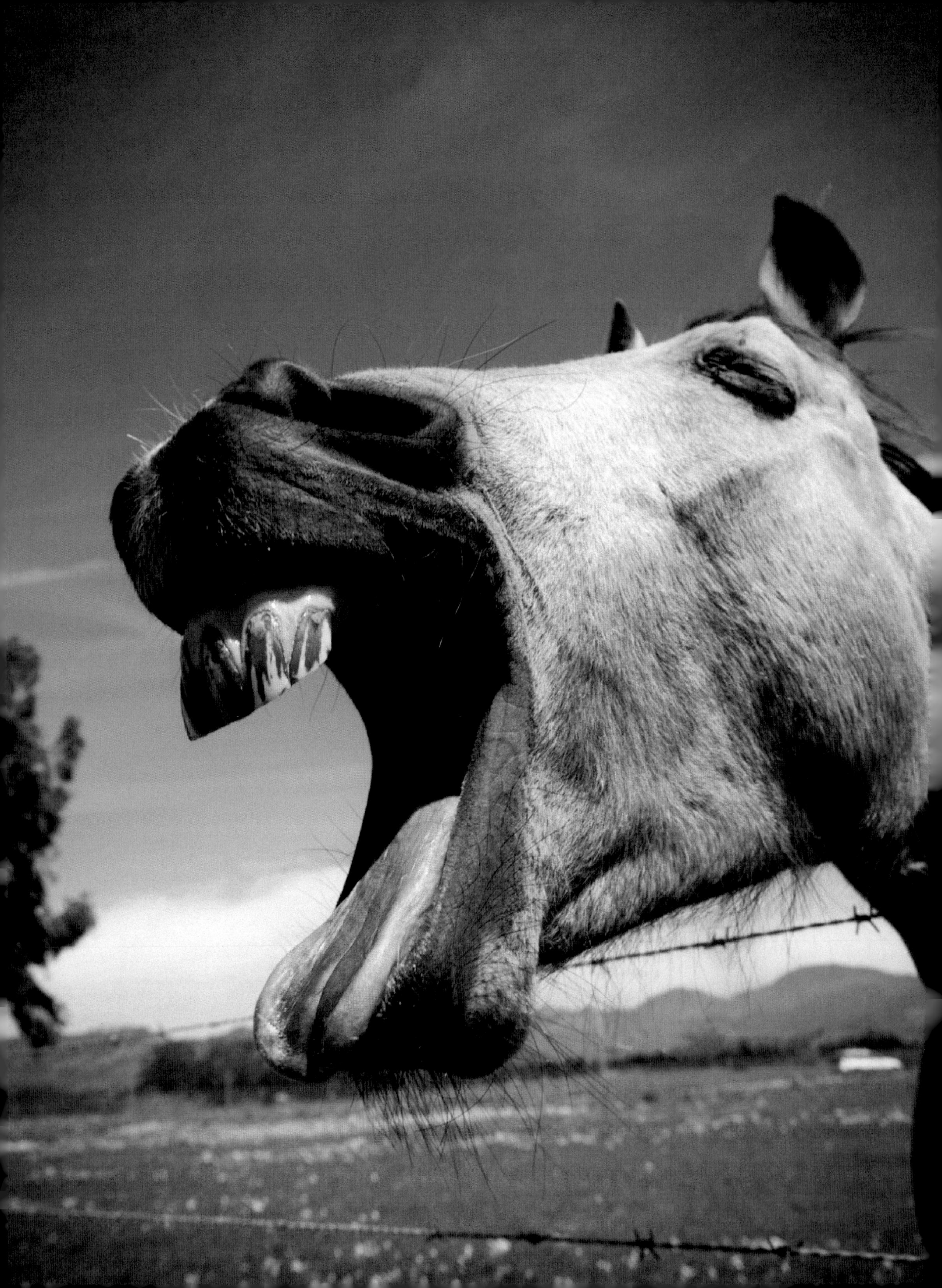

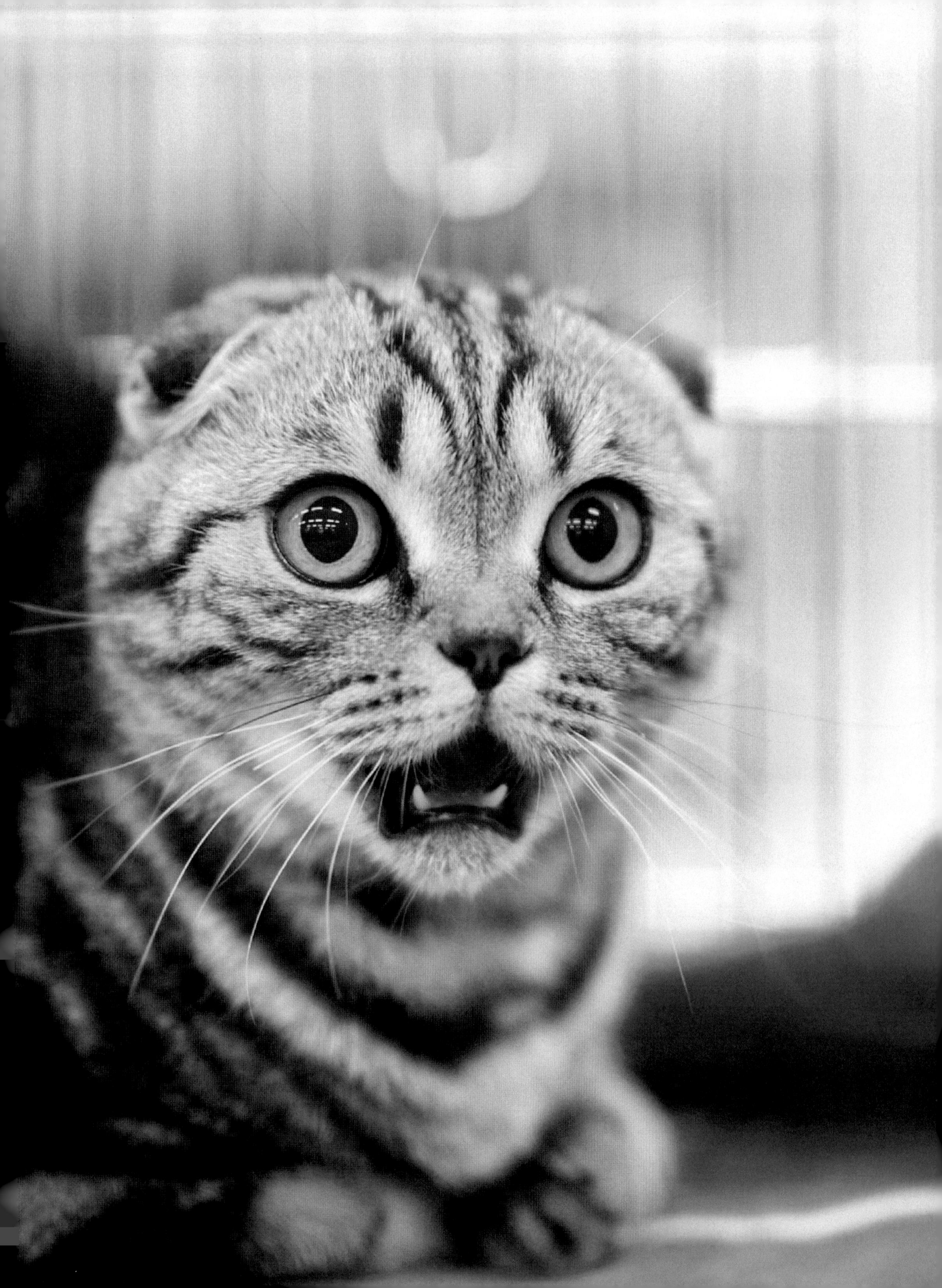

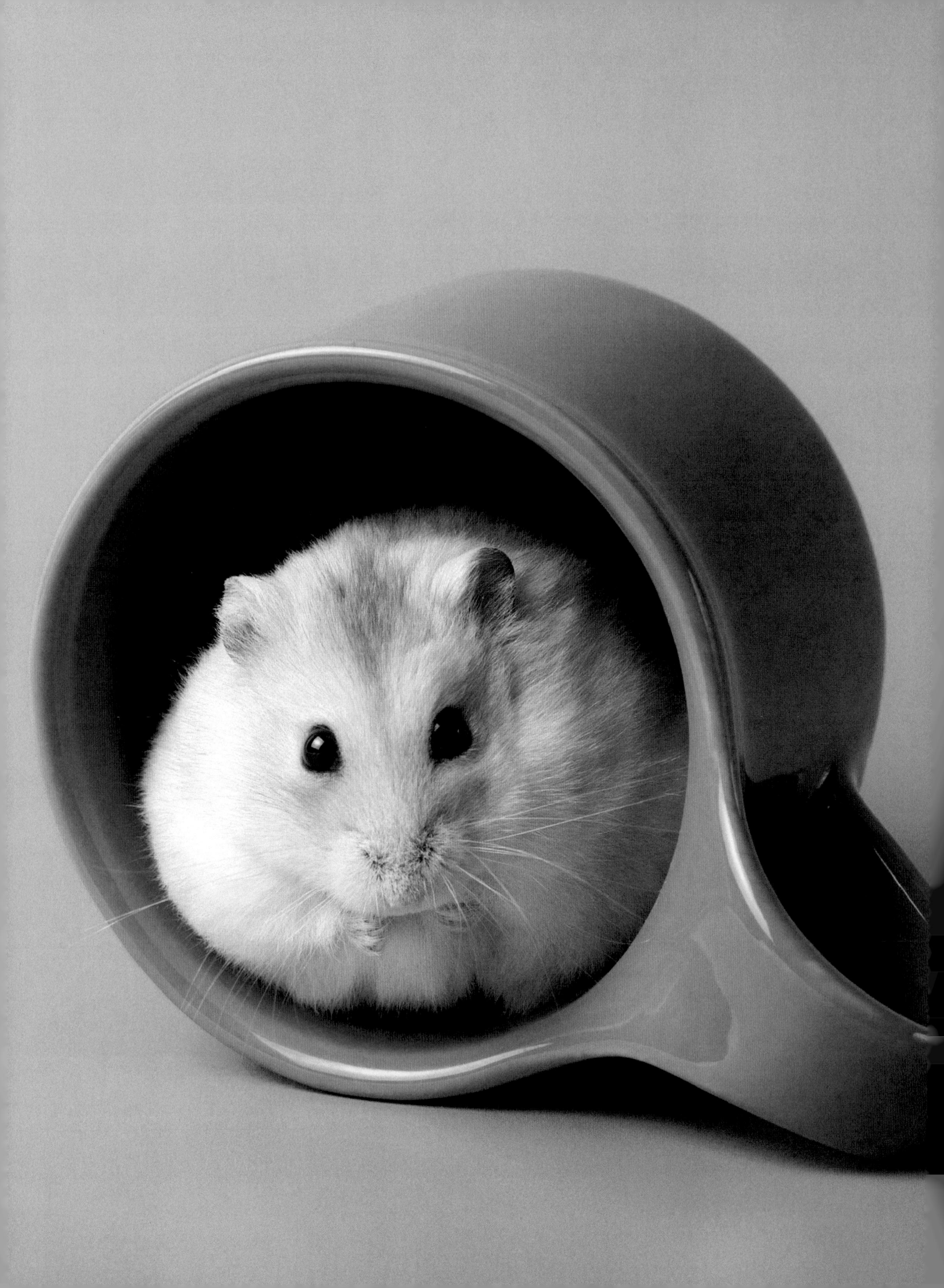

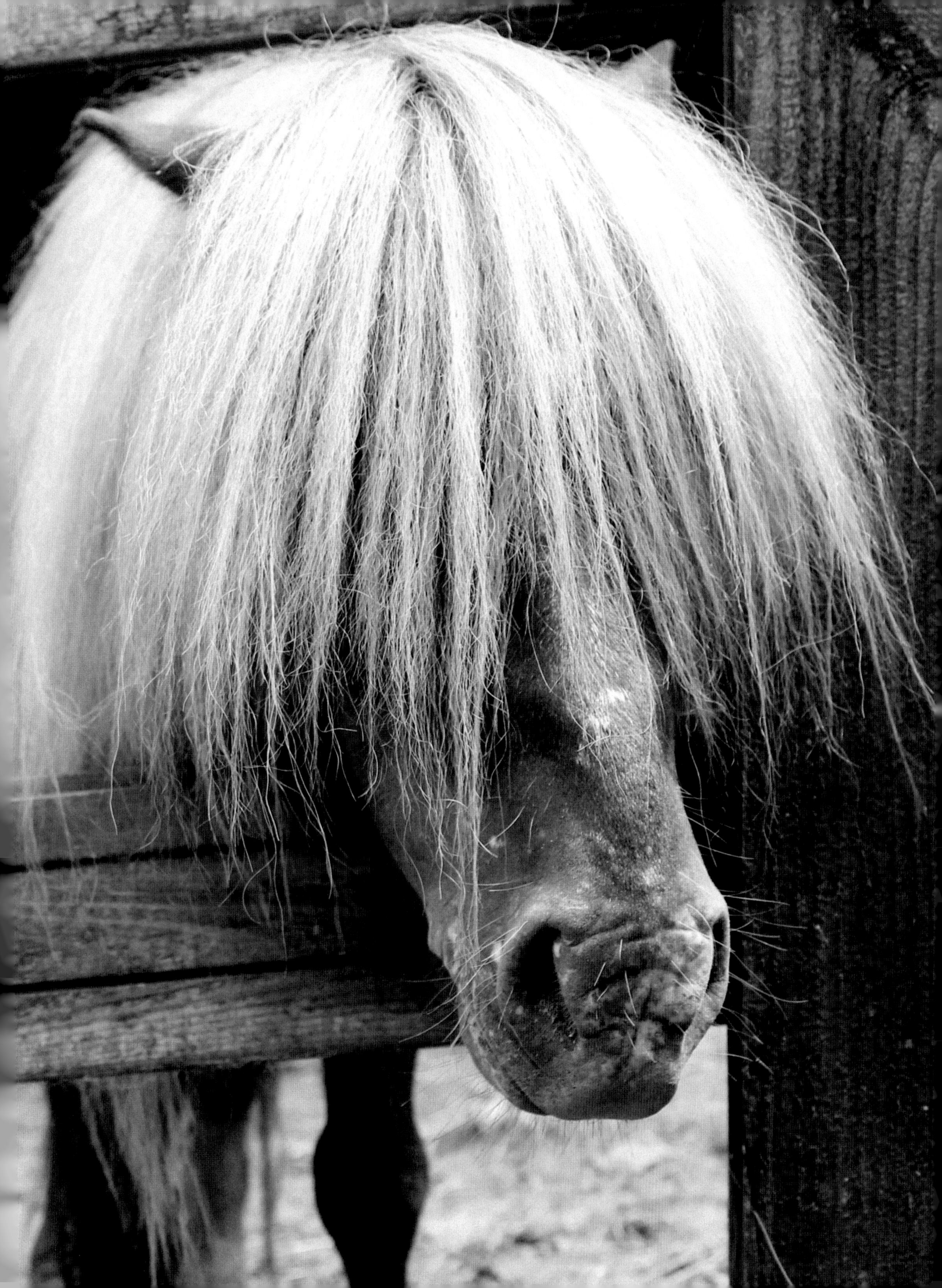

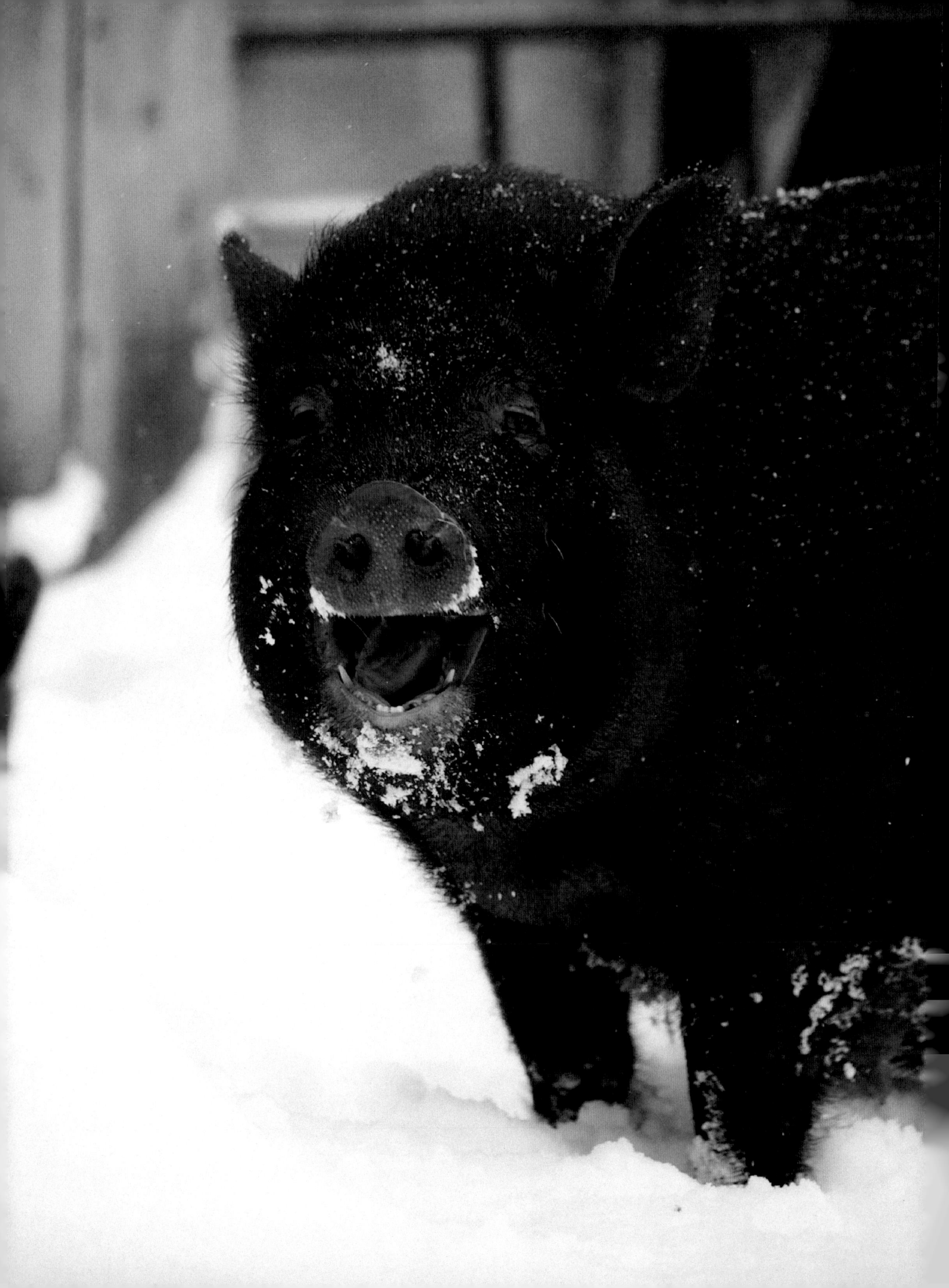

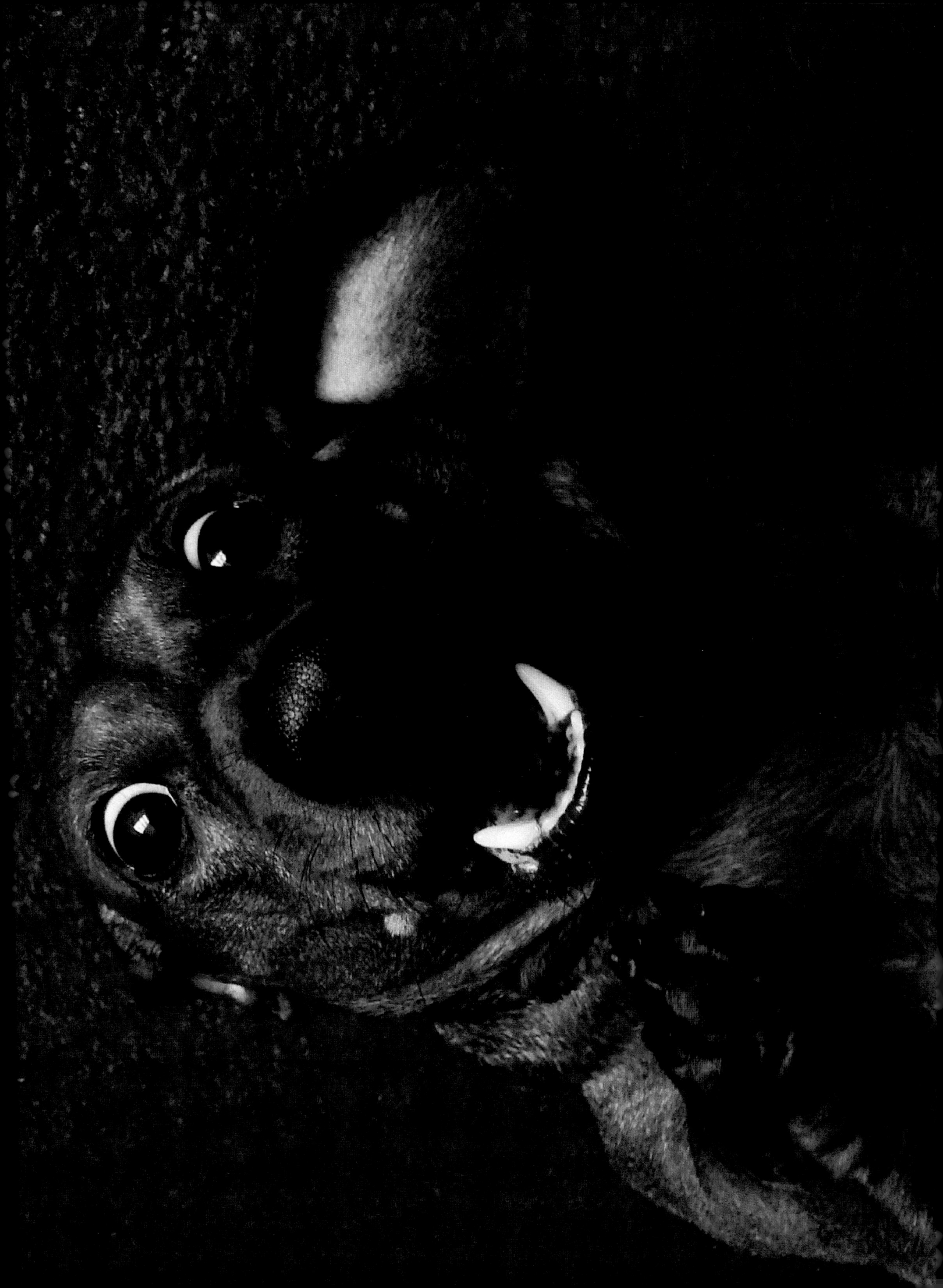

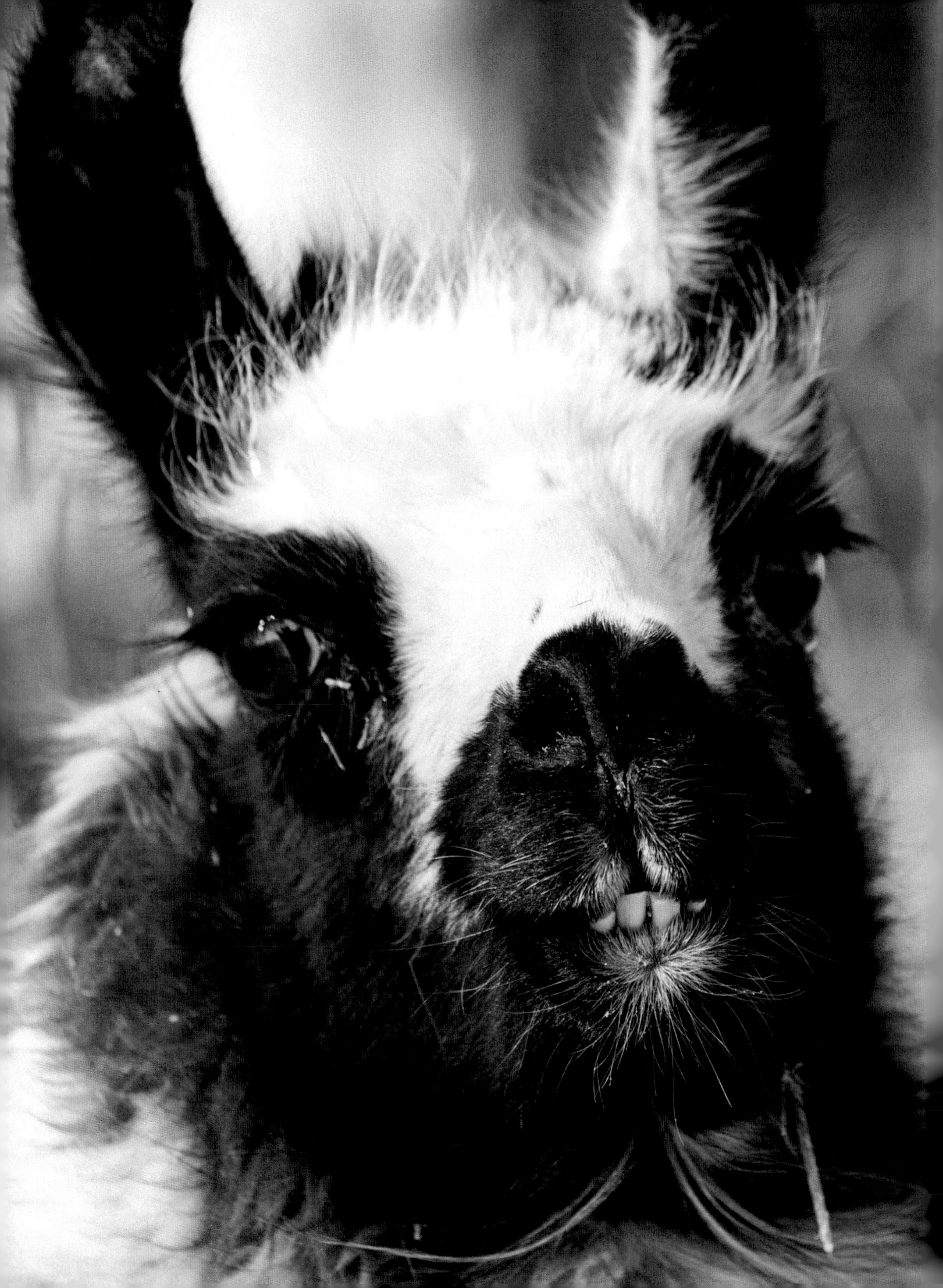

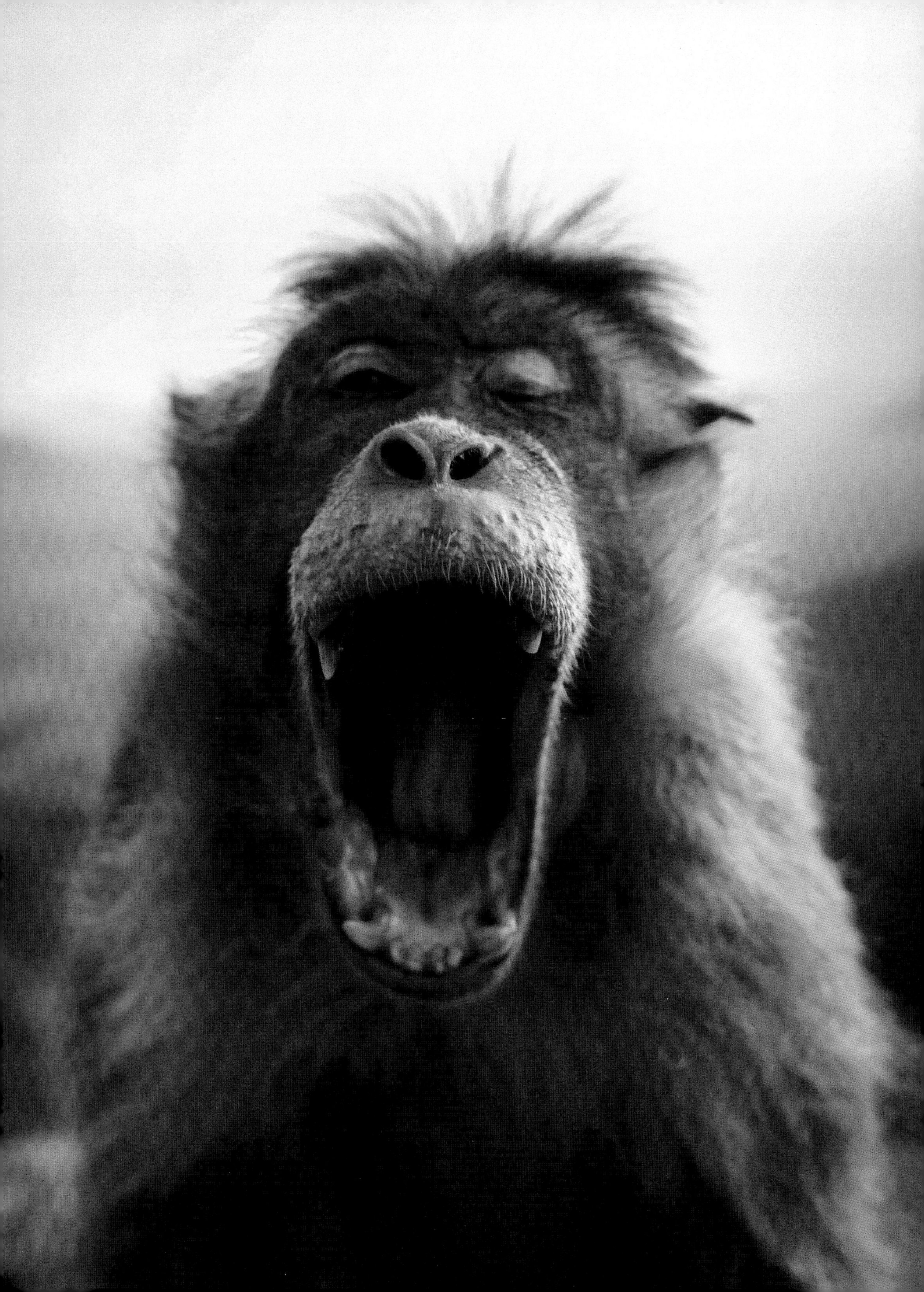

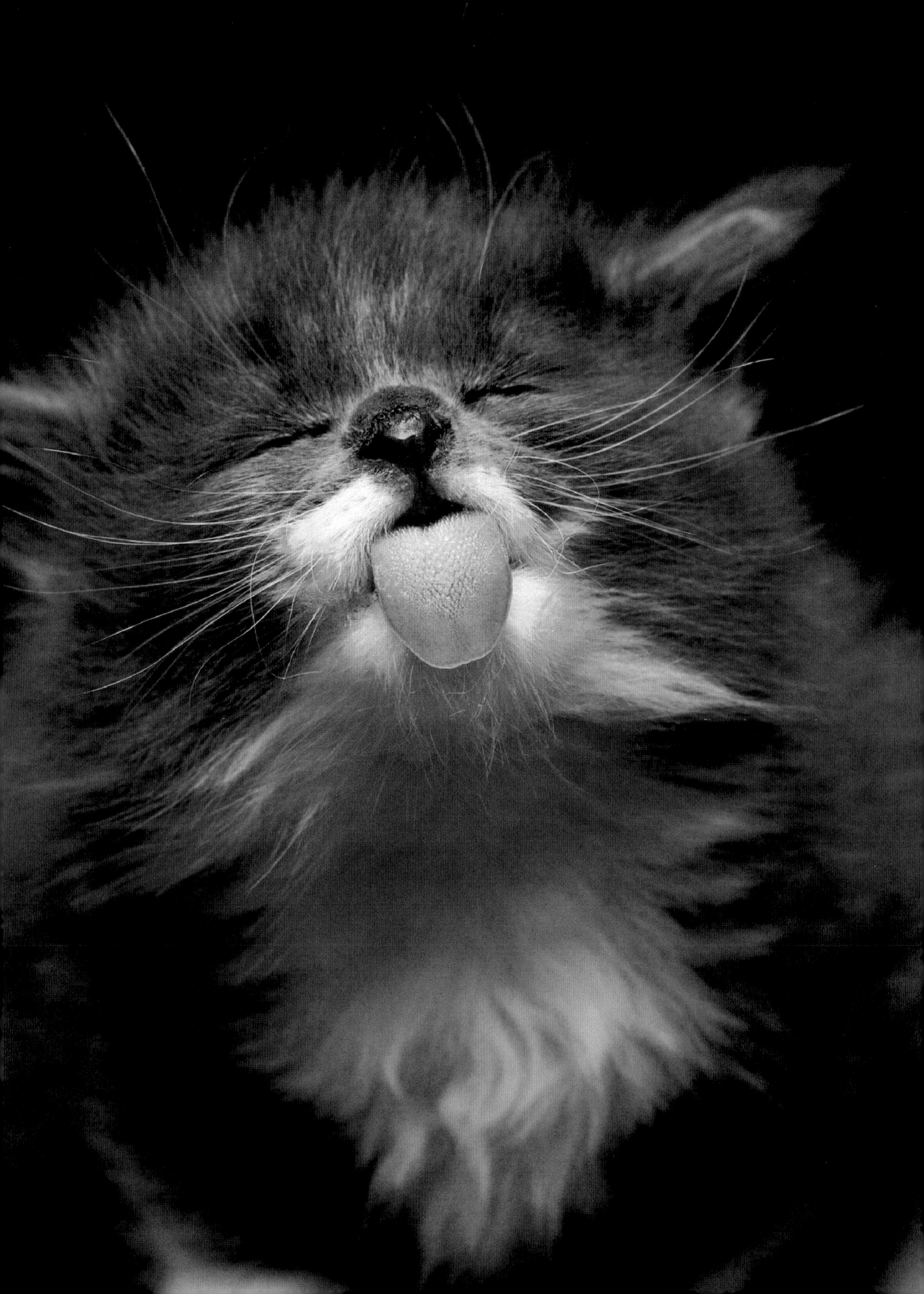